THE COMPREHE~~NSIVE~~

GUIDE TO
MASTERING AI
FOR LEADERS

Master Artificial Intelligence without the Jargon – Your Non-Technical Guidebook for Innovation, Strategy, and Business Growth

Silva Nash

Dedication

To the visionary leaders embracing innovation—may you harness AI not as a replacement, but as a catalyst for greatness.

And to those who dare to lead in the age of intelligence—may your strategy shape the future.

Why This Book?

The rise of artificial intelligence is transforming industries, businesses, and leadership at an unprecedented pace. Leaders who fail to adapt risk falling behind, but navigating AI can feel overwhelming—especially for those without a technical background. That's where this book comes in. Designed specifically for non-technical leaders, this guide breaks down the complexities of AI into practical, easy-to-understand strategies that drive innovation and enhance decision-making. Whether you're looking to improve operational efficiency, gain a competitive edge, or future-proof your organization, this book equips you with the knowledge and tools to harness AI's full potential. You'll learn how to integrate AI into your daily workflow, automate tasks for maximum productivity, and leverage data-driven insights to make smarter, faster decisions. Most importantly, this book will help you stay ahead of the curve, ensuring that AI becomes your most valuable asset rather than an intimidating challenge. AI isn't replacing leaders—it's empowering them. The question isn't whether AI will shape the future of leadership, but whether you'll be ready to lead in the AI era. This book ensures that you are.

Table of Contents

INTRODUCTION

The AI Revolution: What It Means for Leaders

The world is undergoing one of the most profound technological transformations in history. Artificial Intelligence (AI) is no longer a futuristic concept confined to the pages of science fiction. It is here, actively reshaping industries, redefining job roles, and fundamentally altering the way organizations operate. From automating repetitive tasks to providing deep insights through data analytics, AI has become an indispensable tool for businesses worldwide.

For leaders, this revolution presents both an opportunity and a challenge. The opportunity lies in leveraging AI to enhance efficiency, drive innovation, and make more informed decisions. The challenge, however, is in understanding how to integrate AI seamlessly into leadership strategies while ensuring ethical considerations and human oversight remain at the forefront. Those who fail to adapt risk being left behind in an increasingly AI-driven world.

Leaders must recognize that AI is not here to replace them but to augment their capabilities. The most successful executives, managers, and business owners of the future will be those who understand how to work alongside AI, using it to enhance their decision-making processes rather than fearing its implications. This book is designed to help you do exactly that—to demystify AI, equip you with practical tools, and position you at the forefront of the AI-driven leadership revolution.

Embracing AI as a Tool for Strategic Advantage

As a leader, your primary goal is to create value for your organization, employees, and stakeholders. AI provides a powerful means to do so by enhancing productivity, streamlining operations, and offering insights that would be impossible to obtain through traditional methods. Whether you lead a small startup or a multinational corporation, understanding AI's role in business strategy is critical.

One of the key ways AI is revolutionizing leadership is through data-driven decision-making. AI can process vast amounts of data in seconds, identifying patterns and trends that humans might overlook. This capability allows leaders to make more accurate predictions, optimize resource allocation, and anticipate market shifts before they happen. Instead of relying solely on intuition or past experiences, AI enables leaders to base their decisions on real-time, actionable insights.

Another major advantage of AI is its ability to automate repetitive and time-consuming tasks. Many leadership roles require handling administrative duties, scheduling, and communication. AI-powered tools can take over these functions, freeing up leaders to focus on high-value strategic thinking, innovation, and team engagement. Imagine an AI assistant that automatically schedules meetings based on participants' availability, drafts emails based on past communication styles, or even generates reports with actionable recommendations. These advancements are not just theoretical; they are already transforming how modern leaders operate.

However, AI is not just about efficiency; it is also a powerful tool for fostering creativity and innovation. AI-driven analytics can help organizations identify untapped market opportunities, optimize product development, and even personalize customer experiences at an unprecedented scale. Leaders who embrace AI as a tool for strategic advantage will find themselves at the forefront of business innovation, while those who resist may struggle to keep up.

Despite its numerous advantages, AI also presents challenges. Ethical concerns, data privacy issues, and the risk of over-reliance on automation must be carefully managed. As a leader, it is your responsibility to ensure that AI is used responsibly, ethically, and transparently within your organization. This book will guide you through the best practices for ethical

AI implementation, helping you balance technological advancements with human-centric leadership.

Overview of the Book's Structure and How to Use It

This book is structured to provide a comprehensive understanding of AI for leaders, whether you are a seasoned executive or just beginning your journey in AI adoption. The goal is to make AI accessible, actionable, and applicable to your daily leadership responsibilities. Each chapter is designed to build upon the previous one, gradually equipping you with the knowledge and skills needed to integrate AI into your leadership strategy effectively.

Part 1: Understanding AI for Leaders

The first section of the book lays the foundation by breaking down AI into simple, understandable concepts. It covers:

- The fundamentals of AI, machine learning, and large language models (LLMs)
- Key AI terms and technologies every leader should know
- Practical tools and software that can enhance leadership efficiency
- How AI-powered assistants, such as Microsoft Copilot, can transform workplace productivity

Part 2: Practical Applications of AI in Leadership

Once you understand the basics, the next step is to see AI in action. This section explores:

- Real-world AI applications in decision-making, communication, and operations
- How AI enhances content creation, business intelligence, and financial forecasting

- The role of AI in improving team management and organizational productivity
- Practical case studies from successful AI-driven companies

Part 3: Integrating AI into Your Organization

Adopting AI is not just about using new tools; it requires a cultural and operational shift. This part of the book provides a roadmap for:

- Implementing AI strategically across different business functions
- Training and upskilling employees to work alongside AI
- Developing an AI adoption plan tailored to your organization's needs
- Measuring the return on investment (ROI) of AI initiatives

Part 4: AI Ethics, Security, and the Future of Leadership

AI's rapid evolution raises ethical and security concerns. As a leader, it is crucial to navigate these challenges responsibly. This section delves into:

- The importance of ethical AI use and bias mitigation
- Data privacy laws and compliance considerations
- Strategies for ensuring AI aligns with corporate values and mission
- Preparing for the future of AI in leadership roles

Each chapter includes practical insights, real-life examples, and actionable steps that you can implement immediately. Additionally, at the end of the book, you will find a glossary of AI terms, a list of recommended AI tools, and resources for further learning.

How to Get the Most Out of This Book

This book is designed to be a hands-on guide rather than just a theoretical discussion of AI. To maximize its value:

- **Read actively**: Take notes, highlight key concepts, and think about how AI applies to your specific leadership role.
- **Experiment with AI tools**: Throughout the book, we discuss various AI-powered applications. Try them out to see their impact firsthand.
- **Engage your team**: AI adoption is most successful when it is a collective effort. Share insights with colleagues and encourage discussions about AI's role in your organization.
- **Apply what you learn**: Each chapter includes actionable takeaways. Implement these strategies step by step to integrate AI effectively into your leadership approach.

By the time you finish this book, you will not only understand AI but also be equipped to leverage it as a strategic advantage in your leadership journey. AI is not just the future—it is the present. The leaders who embrace it today will be the visionaries of tomorrow. Welcome to the AI-driven era of leadership. Let's begin.

PART 1: UNDERSTANDING AI FOR LEADERS

CHAPTER 1: WELCOME TO THE AGE OF AI FOR LEADERS

AI-Powered Leadership: The Future is Now

We are living in an era where artificial intelligence (AI) is no longer a futuristic concept—it's a fundamental force driving business, governance, and innovation. Leaders today are not just responsible for managing people and resources; they must also navigate an AI-driven landscape that continuously evolves, bringing new opportunities and challenges.

AI is transforming industries at an unprecedented rate. From automation to data analytics, predictive modelling to enhanced decision-making, AI is empowering leaders to make more informed, data-driven choices. Organizations that fail to integrate AI into their strategy risk falling behind, while those that harness its power will thrive in this fast-changing world.

Leadership in the AI era is not about replacing human intelligence but amplifying it. The most successful leaders today are those who embrace AI as a tool for enhancing productivity, optimizing business operations, and driving innovation. Whether in finance, healthcare, marketing, or government, AI-powered leadership is the key to staying competitive.

Understanding Why AI is Not a Threat, But a Partner

One of the biggest misconceptions about AI is that it is here to replace human jobs. The reality is far more nuanced. AI is not a threat; it's a collaborator that enhances our ability to lead effectively. AI excels in handling repetitive tasks, processing vast amounts of data in seconds, and identifying patterns that might take humans years to recognize.

Consider AI-driven automation in businesses—mundane and time-consuming tasks like scheduling, data entry, and customer inquiries are now managed by AI-powered tools. This frees up valuable time for leaders to focus on strategic decision-making, team development, and innovation.

Leaders who embrace AI as a strategic partner will find themselves more empowered, not less. AI provides enhanced insights, helps mitigate risks, and enables faster, more efficient operations. Instead of replacing leadership, AI augments it by offering predictive analytics, intelligent automation, and real-time decision-making support.

How AI is Reshaping the Leadership Landscape

AI is not just changing how we work—it is redefining leadership itself. Leaders today must adopt a new mindset—one that values agility, continuous learning, and a willingness to adapt.

1. **Data-Driven Decision Making**

    AI has given leaders access to real-time insights that were once impossible to gather manually. Predictive analytics allow leaders to anticipate market trends, customer behavior, and operational risks with unprecedented accuracy. A CEO today doesn't have to rely solely on gut instinct; AI-driven analytics provide a foundation for more informed, evidence-based decisions.

2. **Personalized Leadership at Scale**

    Managing a large workforce has always been a challenge, but AI has introduced new ways to personalize leadership at scale. AI-driven tools can analyze employee performance, engagement, and well-being, helping leaders understand individual and team dynamics better. This means more effective leadership strategies tailored to the unique needs of employees.

3. **Enhanced Productivity and Efficiency**

    AI-driven automation eliminates inefficiencies in workflow management, allowing leaders to focus on high-impact tasks. AI tools optimize project management, customer interactions, and operational logistics, helping organizations maximize output with fewer resources.

4. **Ethical AI Leadership**

    As AI takes on a larger role in decision-making, ethical considerations become more critical than ever. Leaders must ensure AI applications are used responsibly, avoiding bias, protecting data privacy, and maintaining transparency. Ethical AI leadership requires a commitment to fairness, accountability, and trust-building.

5. **AI and Human Collaboration**

    The best organizations are those where AI and human employees work together harmoniously. AI enhances creativity, problem-solving, and innovation, but it still requires human oversight and ethical judgment. Leaders must create environments where AI and human intelligence complement each other rather than compete.

The age of AI is here, and it demands a new breed of leadership. The leaders who thrive in this new era will not be those who resist AI but those who embrace it as a powerful partner. AI is not a threat to leadership; it is a force multiplier that amplifies human intelligence, enhances decision-making, and drives business success.

As you move forward in this book, you will learn how to integrate AI into your leadership strategy, leverage its potential for innovation, and navigate the ethical and practical challenges it presents. The future belongs to leaders who understand that AI is not just a tool—it's a transformative force that will shape the next generation of leadership.

CHAPTER 2: DEMYSTIFYING AI – BUILDING YOUR LEADERSHIP TECH VOCABULARY

Artificial Intelligence (AI) has become one of the most transformative forces in the modern business world, reshaping industries, streamlining operations, and unlocking new opportunities for innovation. However, for many leaders, AI can feel like an overwhelming and highly technical domain, filled with jargon that makes it difficult to grasp its true potential.

The good news is that you don't need to be a data scientist or software engineer to understand AI. As a leader, your role is to harness AI's power strategically, ensuring that it aligns with your organization's goals and creates real value. To do that, you need a strong foundation in AI fundamentals, an understanding of how AI works, and the ability to communicate effectively with technical teams.

This chapter will demystify AI, breaking it down into easy-to-understand concepts, providing real-world examples, and introducing the key terminology that every leader should know. By the end of this chapter, you'll be able to engage confidently in AI discussions, identify areas where AI can enhance your business, and bridge the gap between technical experts and business decision-making.

The Core Concepts and Essence of AI

At its core, Artificial Intelligence is about enabling machines to mimic human intelligence. This means AI systems can analyze data, recognize patterns, make predictions, and even take actions based on what they've learned. But how does AI actually work?

To truly understand AI, let's break it down into some fundamental concepts that power this revolutionary technology.

Machine Learning (ML) – Teaching AI to Learn from Data

One of the most important aspects of AI is Machine Learning (ML). Machine learning allows computers to learn from vast amounts of data, identify patterns, and improve their performance over time—without needing to be explicitly programmed for every scenario.

Imagine a customer service AI that answers support questions. Instead of programming the AI with thousands of specific answers, the AI is trained on a massive dataset of customer inquiries and responses. Over time, it learns the best way to respond based on previous successful interactions.

Here's a real-world example: Netflix's recommendation system. When you watch a show or movie, Netflix's AI learns your preferences and suggests content you're likely to enjoy. The more you watch, the smarter it gets because it continuously learns from your viewing habits.

Machine learning is the backbone of AI applications, powering everything from fraud detection in banking to personalized marketing campaigns and even medical diagnoses.

Understanding the Building Blocks of AI Technology

AI doesn't just work magically—it relies on specific building blocks that allow it to function effectively. As a leader, knowing these essential components will help you make informed decisions about AI integration in your organization.

1. Algorithms – The Rules That AI Follows

An algorithm is a set of instructions that an AI system follows to process data and make decisions. Think of an algorithm as the recipe that guides AI on how to analyze information and generate results.

For example, when you search for something on Google, an AI algorithm determines which search results are the most relevant based on your query. Similarly, AI-powered fraud detection in banks uses algorithms to spot unusual spending behavior, flagging suspicious transactions for further investigation.

Understanding that AI relies on algorithms helps leaders see AI not as magic, but as a structured approach to solving problems efficiently.

2. Data – The Fuel That Powers AI

AI is only as good as the data it is trained on. Without data, AI cannot learn or make intelligent decisions. The quality, quantity, and diversity of data determine how effective an AI system will be.

For instance, AI-powered recruitment tools analyze thousands of resumes to identify the best candidates for a job. However, if the AI is trained on biased data—such as past hiring decisions that favored a certain demographic—the system will replicate that bias, leading to unfair hiring practices.

As a leader, ensuring that your AI systems are trained on accurate, diverse, and high-quality data is crucial for achieving ethical and effective outcomes.

3. Automation – AI's Role in Streamlining Workflows

AI is a game-changer when it comes to automating repetitive tasks and increasing efficiency. Many businesses now rely on AI-powered automation to handle tasks that were previously time-consuming and labor-intensive.

For example:

In HR departments, AI automates resume screening, scheduling interviews, and onboarding new employees.

In marketing, AI generates personalized email campaigns based on customer behavior.

In manufacturing, AI-powered robots streamline production processes and improve quality control.

Automation allows companies to reduce costs, enhance productivity, and free up human employees to focus on higher-value tasks.

AI Glossary for Non-Technical Leaders

To effectively engage in AI discussions, leaders need to be familiar with key AI terminology. Here are some of the most important terms you should know:

Artificial Intelligence (AI)

AI refers to machines that can perform tasks that typically require human intelligence, such as decision-making, learning, and problem-solving.

Example: AI chatbots like ChatGPT that can understand and respond to natural language conversations.

Machine Learning (ML)

A subset of AI that enables machines to learn from data and improve their performance over time without being explicitly programmed.

Example: Google's AI predicting what you're about to type in the search bar based on previous searches.

Deep Learning

A more advanced form of machine learning that mimics the way the human brain processes information using neural networks.

Example: Self-driving cars using deep learning to recognize pedestrians, traffic lights, and road signs.

Natural Language Processing (NLP)

A field of AI that enables computers to understand, interpret, and generate human language.

Example: AI assistants like Siri and Alexa processing voice commands to provide information or complete tasks.

Big Data

Extremely large and complex datasets that AI systems analyze to extract insights and make predictions.

Example: AI in healthcare analyzing millions of patient records to predict disease outbreaks.

By mastering these key AI concepts, leaders can bridge the gap between technology and business strategy, enabling them to make informed decisions about AI adoption.

AI is no longer a futuristic concept—it's a present-day reality that is reshaping the way businesses operate. Leaders who embrace AI will have a significant competitive advantage, while those who ignore it risk being left behind.

The key takeaway from this chapter is that AI is not just for engineers or data scientists. As a leader, understanding AI's core concepts, its building blocks, and how it can be applied in business will empower you to make informed decisions and drive AI-powered innovation.

In the next chapter, we will explore how AI is transforming industries, from healthcare and finance to retail and manufacturing. Get ready to see real-world case studies and discover how you can position your organization for AI success.

The future of AI-driven leadership starts now!

CHAPTER 3: THE AI TOOLKIT FOR LEADERS — WHAT YOU NEED TO KNOW

Artificial intelligence (AI) has evolved from a futuristic concept to an essential tool that every leader must understand and leverage. However, navigating the complex AI landscape can be overwhelming, especially for non-technical leaders. What tools should you focus on? How can you use AI to enhance decision-making and business strategy?

This chapter provides an in-depth exploration of the AI toolkit for leaders, covering the key tools, technologies, and strategies that will empower you to harness AI effectively. Whether you're leading a small startup or a Fortune 500 company, understanding and applying AI in a strategic manner will give you a competitive advantage.

Navigating the AI Landscape: Key Tools and Technologies

To integrate AI successfully into your leadership approach, it's essential to know the tools that power modern AI applications. AI is a vast field, but for business leaders, three categories of AI tools matter most:

1. AI Assistants and Automation Tools
2. Large Language Models (LLMs) and Conversational AI
3. AI-Powered Analytics and Decision-Making Platforms

Let's break them down in detail.

AI Assistants and Automation Tools

AI-powered assistants have revolutionized how leaders manage their time, streamline workflows, and optimize productivity. These tools help automate repetitive tasks, organize information, and even generate strategic insights.

Examples of AI Assistants for Leaders

- Microsoft Copilot – Integrated into Office 365, Copilot assists with drafting emails, summarizing reports, and generating presentations.
- ChatGPT (by OpenAI) – A powerful conversational AI that can help with brainstorming, content creation, and answering complex questions.
- Grammarly AI – Enhances writing by offering AI-driven grammar and style suggestions.
- Notion AI – Automates note-taking, meeting summaries, and project management tasks.
- Zapier AI – Connects apps and automates workflows without needing complex programming.

For leaders, AI assistants enhance productivity, save time, and allow you to focus on strategic decision-making rather than administrative tasks.

Mastering Large Language Models (LLMs) for Effective Communication

One of the most powerful AI tools available today is Large Language Models (LLMs). These AI models are designed to process and generate human-like text, making them invaluable for communication, research, and knowledge management.

What Are LLMs and Why Should Leaders Care?

LLMs, such as GPT-4 (ChatGPT), Google Gemini, and Claude AI, are trained on vast amounts of text data and can:

- Generate reports, emails, and business plans with human-like fluency
- Summarize complex information into concise insights
- Assist in strategic brainstorming and problem-solving
- Translate languages and interpret cultural nuances in communication

How Leaders Can Leverage LLMs

- Drafting Business Documents: AI can quickly generate proposals, summaries, and presentations.
- Enhancing Customer Engagement: AI chatbots can handle customer queries, freeing up human teams.
- Training and Onboarding: AI can create training materials and answer employee FAQs.

Real-World Example

Airbnb uses AI-powered chatbots to assist customers in finding accommodations, handling inquiries, and providing travel recommendations. This has improved customer satisfaction while reducing operational costs.

By mastering LLMs, leaders can enhance communication, streamline operations, and improve decision-making.

Leveraging AI for Data-Driven Decision-Making

Modern leadership relies on data-driven insights rather than intuition alone. AI enhances this process by analyzing vast datasets, identifying patterns, and generating actionable insights.

Key AI Tools for Data Analysis and Decision-Making

- Google Cloud AI & AWS AI – AI-powered cloud platforms that process large-scale business data.
- Power BI & Tableau AI – AI-driven analytics tools that transform raw data into visual insights.
- IBM Watson AI – An advanced AI system used for predictive analytics and business intelligence.

These tools help leaders make more informed, data-backed decisions in real time.

How AI Enhances Decision-Making

- Predictive Analytics: AI can forecast market trends, helping businesses anticipate customer needs.
- Risk Assessment: AI detects fraud and security threats by identifying unusual patterns.
- Personalized Marketing: AI analyzes consumer behavior to create highly targeted campaigns.

Example

Coca-Cola uses AI-powered data analytics to optimize supply chain management, ensuring efficient inventory control and reducing waste.

By integrating AI into decision-making, leaders can increase efficiency, reduce risks, and drive business growth.

The AI revolution is here, and leaders who embrace AI-powered tools will have a significant strategic advantage. Understanding AI assistants, Large Language Models, and AI-driven analytics will enable you to communicate effectively, automate tasks, and make data-driven decisions.

In the next chapter, we will explore how AI is transforming leadership roles and reshaping industries across the world. Now is the time to adopt AI as a partner, not a threat—and use it to drive your business forward!

Understanding ChatGPT and Other AI Communication Tools

In the modern business landscape, AI-driven communication tools are becoming indispensable for leaders. As organizations seek more efficient ways to manage workflows, enhance customer engagement, and optimize decision-making, artificial intelligence—particularly ChatGPT—is proving to be a transformative tool. Leaders who embrace AI-powered communication gain a competitive edge, allowing them to streamline operations, improve productivity, and drive innovation in their industries.

This section delves into ChatGPT's role in business, how it works, and how leaders can use it effectively. We'll explore real-world examples, best practices, and complementary AI tools that can elevate business success.

What is ChatGPT?

ChatGPT, developed by OpenAI, is an advanced conversational AI model that can generate human-like responses to text-based inputs. It leverages deep learning and natural language processing (NLP) to understand context, process vast amounts of information, and generate responses that mimic human communication.

Unlike traditional chatbots that rely on pre-programmed scripts, ChatGPT is dynamic and adaptive, making it ideal for complex business interactions. It can:

- Provide instant responses to customer inquiries.
- Generate reports, emails, and business proposals.
- Assist with brainstorming and problem-solving.
- Translate and interpret complex information.

For leaders, this means a more efficient way to manage communication, optimize decision-making, and enhance customer and employee interactions.

How ChatGPT Enhances Business Performance

Leaders across industries are using ChatGPT to drive business efficiency and innovation. Below are key areas where ChatGPT is making a significant impact.

1. Customer Support and Engagement

Companies are increasingly integrating ChatGPT into their customer service operations. AI-powered chatbots provide:

- 24/7 instant responses to customer inquiries.
- Personalized assistance based on user data.
- Consistent and accurate information delivery.

Example: E-commerce Industry

Online retailers like Shopify-powered stores use ChatGPT-driven chatbots to handle customer queries, recommend products, and process refunds. This reduces wait times and enhances customer satisfaction, ultimately increasing sales.

2. Content Creation and Marketing

Content is crucial for brand visibility and engagement. ChatGPT helps businesses generate:

- Blog posts, articles, and social media content.
- SEO-optimized website copy.
- Personalized email marketing campaigns.

Example: Digital Marketing Agencies

Marketing firms use ChatGPT to generate high-quality blog posts and ad copies. Agencies like HubSpot employ AI-driven tools to personalize marketing efforts, leading to higher engagement rates.

3. Data Analysis and Business Insights

Leaders rely on data-driven decisions, but analyzing large datasets can be time-consuming. ChatGPT can:

- Summarize complex reports into actionable insights.
- Analyze customer feedback and generate sentiment analysis.
- Provide quick interpretations of financial and market data.

Example: Financial Services

Investment firms use ChatGPT to automate reports, summarize financial trends, and generate insights on stock performance. A hedge fund manager, for instance, can use AI to sift through thousands of reports and identify profitable investment opportunities.

4. Human Resource Management and Recruitment

Recruitment is a crucial function that AI is transforming. ChatGPT can:

- Automate resume screening.
- Conduct initial interview assessments.
- Generate employee training materials.

Example: HR Tech Companies

Companies like Workday and BambooHR integrate AI-driven tools to streamline hiring. ChatGPT-powered bots conduct initial candidate assessments, reducing recruitment time by up to 50%.

5. Sales and Lead Generation

Sales teams use AI-driven communication tools to optimize lead generation and conversion. ChatGPT helps by:

- Personalizing outreach messages.
- Automating responses to potential clients.
- Providing instant follow-ups on inquiries.

Example: B2B Sales Companies

Sales teams at Salesforce and HubSpot leverage AI-driven chatbots to nurture leads and automate repetitive sales tasks, increasing conversion rates.

6. Internal Communication and Workflow Automation

Leaders and teams rely on efficient communication to drive business success. ChatGPT assists in:

- Generating meeting summaries and action points.
- Automating responses to frequently asked questions.
- Assisting in project management by tracking deadlines.

Startups use Notion AI, integrated with ChatGPT, to automate documentation and streamline internal workflows. This allows teams to focus on strategic tasks rather than administrative work.

7. Legal and Compliance Support

Businesses must navigate complex legal and compliance landscapes. ChatGPT aids by:

- Summarizing legal documents and contracts.
- Providing instant insights on compliance regulations.
- Assisting in policy documentation.

Example: Corporate Law Firms

Legal firms use AI tools like Harvey AI, powered by ChatGPT, to analyze case law and draft contracts, improving efficiency and reducing legal research time.

Other AI Communication Tools Leaders Should Know

While ChatGPT is a powerful tool, several other AI-driven communication solutions can enhance business operations.

1. Microsoft Copilot

Integrated into Microsoft 365, Copilot enhances productivity by:

- Generating documents and reports.
- Summarizing long email threads.
- Creating PowerPoint presentations.

2. Google Gemini (Formerly Bard)

Google Gemini excels at:

- Providing AI-powered research assistance.
- Automating content creation and email responses.
- Integrating with Google Workspace tools.

3. Claude AI (Anthropic)

Claude AI is known for:

- Ethical and context-aware responses.
- Summarizing extensive documents.
- AI-powered customer support solutions.

4. Notion AI

Notion AI is a productivity tool that:

- Automates note-taking.
- Structures business plans and documentation.
- Streamlines project management.

5. Grammarly AI

Grammarly AI enhances business communication by:

- Improving tone and clarity.
- Providing AI-powered content suggestions.
- Enhancing email and document quality.

Real-World Success Stories

1. AI in Business Strategy

A startup founder uses ChatGPT to draft investor pitch decks, summarize market trends, and refine business strategies—saving hours of manual work.

2. AI in Corporate Communication

A Fortune 500 executive integrates Microsoft Copilot to summarize reports, prioritize emails, and draft clear, concise responses.

3. AI in Leadership Development

A CEO leverages Notion AI to automate employee engagement surveys and structure leadership training materials.

Best Practices for Implementing ChatGPT in Business

1. **Verify AI-Generated Content** – Always review AI responses, especially for critical decisions.
2. **Maintain a Human Touch** – AI should enhance, not replace, human leadership.
3. **Customize AI Outputs** – Train AI tools with business-specific data for improved relevance.
4. **Balance AI and Ethical Use** – Ensure responsible AI implementation to avoid misinformation.

AI-powered communication tools like ChatGPT, Microsoft Copilot, and Google Gemini are revolutionizing leadership and business operations. By understanding and leveraging these tools, leaders can enhance efficiency, improve decision-making, and drive innovation.

The businesses that adapt to AI-driven communication will thrive in the digital economy. Mastering AI-powered tools ensures that leaders remain competitive, making informed, strategic decisions that shape the future of their industries.

Exploring AI's Capabilities in Automation and Efficiency

Artificial Intelligence (AI) has revolutionized the way businesses operate, enabling automation and efficiency at an unprecedented scale. For leaders, AI is not just a tool for convenience; it is a strategic asset that can streamline operations, reduce costs, and enhance productivity. Understanding how AI-driven automation works and how to implement it effectively is critical for staying competitive in the modern business landscape.

This section explores AI's role in automation and efficiency, providing practical examples of how organizations use AI to optimize workflows, improve decision-making, and drive innovation.

The Role of AI in Automation

Automation refers to the use of technology to perform tasks with minimal human intervention. AI-powered automation goes a step further by incorporating machine learning, natural language processing (NLP), and predictive analytics to improve decision-making and task execution dynamically.

AI automation is transforming industries by:

- **Eliminating repetitive tasks** – Reducing manual effort and freeing up employees for strategic roles.
- **Enhancing accuracy** – AI minimizes human errors in data entry, analysis, and decision-making.
- **Increasing speed** – Processes that once took hours or days can be completed in minutes.

- **Improving scalability** – AI-driven automation allows businesses to scale operations without a proportional increase in resources.

Key AI Automation Technologies

1. **Robotic Process Automation (RPA)** – AI-powered bots handle repetitive tasks like data entry, invoice processing, and customer support.
2. **Machine Learning Algorithms** – AI models analyze patterns and make predictions to optimize workflows.
3. **Natural Language Processing (NLP)** – AI understands and processes human language to automate customer interactions, document management, and sentiment analysis.
4. **Computer Vision** – AI recognizes and interprets visual data for quality control, surveillance, and automation in manufacturing.
5. **AI Chatbots and Virtual Assistants** – These tools automate communication, answering customer inquiries and scheduling tasks.

AI-Driven Efficiency: Transforming Business Operations

Leaders who implement AI-driven automation see a dramatic improvement in operational efficiency. Below are key areas where AI enhances productivity and drives business growth.

1. AI in Business Process Automation

AI-powered automation is streamlining workflows across various industries. Businesses use AI-driven tools to:

- Automate payroll processing and HR functions.
- Generate and analyze financial reports.
- Manage supply chain logistics.

Example: Finance Industry

Banks and financial institutions use AI-powered RPA to automate loan processing, fraud detection, and compliance reporting. This not only reduces operational costs but also ensures accuracy and regulatory compliance.

2. AI in Customer Service

AI-powered chatbots and virtual assistants have transformed customer support by providing:

- 24/7 automated customer service.
- Instant responses to common inquiries.
- Personalized recommendations based on customer behavior.

Example: E-commerce

Companies like Amazon and Shopify integrate AI chatbots to handle customer queries, process orders, and provide product recommendations—reducing response times and increasing customer satisfaction.

3. AI in Supply Chain Management

AI enhances supply chain operations by:

- Predicting demand fluctuations to optimize inventory.
- Automating warehouse management through AI-powered robots.
- Reducing waste by analyzing logistics efficiency.

Example: Retail Industry

Walmart uses AI-powered demand forecasting to ensure optimal stock levels, reducing excess inventory and preventing shortages.

4. AI in Human Resources and Recruitment

AI is transforming HR functions by automating:

- Resume screening and candidate shortlisting.
- Employee training through AI-powered learning platforms.
- Performance analysis to identify top talent.

Example: Tech Industry

Companies like IBM use AI-driven recruitment platforms to screen thousands of resumes, significantly reducing hiring time.

5. AI in Healthcare and Diagnostics

AI is revolutionizing healthcare by automating:

- Medical imaging analysis for early disease detection.
- Patient data management and record-keeping.
- Personalized treatment recommendations.

Example: Medical Field

AI-powered systems like IBM Watson assist doctors by analyzing medical records and suggesting treatment plans based on patient history.

6. AI in Manufacturing and Production

AI-driven automation in manufacturing improves:

- Quality control using computer vision.
- Predictive maintenance to prevent equipment failures.
- Robotics-driven assembly lines for faster production.

Tesla uses AI-powered robots to automate vehicle assembly, ensuring precision and efficiency while reducing production time.

7. AI in Sales and Marketing

AI helps businesses optimize sales and marketing efforts by:

- Automating personalized email campaigns.
- Predicting customer preferences using AI analytics.
- Enhancing ad targeting through machine learning.

Example: Digital Marketing

Google Ads uses AI to optimize ad placements, ensuring businesses reach the right audience at the right time.

8. AI in Cybersecurity and Risk Management

AI enhances security by:

- Detecting and preventing cyber threats in real time.
- Automating fraud detection in financial transactions.
- Monitoring networks for suspicious activity.

Example: Cybersecurity Firms

Companies like Darktrace use AI-powered threat detection to safeguard businesses from cyberattacks.

Overcoming Challenges in AI Automation

Despite its benefits, AI-driven automation comes with challenges, including:

- **Job displacement concerns** – Employees fear AI will replace human jobs. Solution: Upskilling and reskilling employees to work alongside AI.
- **Implementation costs** – AI integration can be expensive. Solution: Phased implementation and leveraging cloud-based AI solutions.
- **Data privacy risks** – AI systems rely on large datasets, raising privacy concerns. Solution: Adopting ethical AI practices and compliance measures.

Best Practices for Implementing AI Automation

1. **Identify automation opportunities** – Focus on repetitive, high-volume tasks that AI can optimize.
2. **Ensure data quality** – AI thrives on accurate, well-structured data.
3. **Train employees** – Equip teams with AI skills to maximize efficiency.
4. **Monitor AI performance** – Regularly evaluate AI-driven processes to refine automation strategies.

AI is redefining business operations, enabling automation and efficiency across industries. Leaders who embrace AI-driven automation not only optimize productivity but also future-proof their organizations against evolving market demands.

By leveraging AI tools strategically, businesses can enhance operational efficiency, reduce costs, and create more innovative, customer-centric solutions. The key is to view AI not as a replacement for human talent, but as an enabler of smarter, faster, and more efficient decision-making.

Harnessing Microsoft Copilot for Productivity and Innovation

Artificial Intelligence has become a cornerstone of modern business strategy, enabling leaders to drive efficiency, innovation, and competitive advantage. One of the most transformative AI-driven tools for business leaders today is Microsoft Copilot—a powerful AI assistant designed to seamlessly integrate into Microsoft's ecosystem, enhancing productivity, automating workflows, and enabling smarter decision-making.

Microsoft Copilot is more than just an AI assistant; it represents a shift in how professionals interact with technology, offering a context-aware, adaptive, and intelligent system that enhances daily tasks. From writing and summarizing emails to generating insights from large datasets, Copilot empowers leaders to work smarter, not harder.

This section explores how business leaders can leverage Microsoft Copilot to enhance productivity, foster innovation, and streamline operations.

What is Microsoft Copilot?

Microsoft Copilot is an AI-powered assistant that integrates with Microsoft 365 applications, including Word, Excel, PowerPoint, Outlook, Teams, and more. It uses advanced machine learning and natural language processing (NLP) to understand user intent and provide contextually relevant assistance.

Unlike traditional automation tools, Copilot learns from user behavior, making it a dynamic and intelligent AI partner rather than just a rule-based assistant.

Key Features of Microsoft Copilot

1. **Seamless Integration with Microsoft 365** – Copilot works within Word, Excel, PowerPoint, Teams, and Outlook, offering real-time assistance.
2. **AI-Powered Writing and Editing** – Copilot can generate reports, emails, and presentations with human-like fluency.
3. **Data Analysis and Insights** – In Excel, Copilot can analyze trends, generate visualizations, and provide actionable insights.

4. **Automated Meeting Summaries** – In Microsoft Teams, Copilot can generate real-time meeting transcriptions and action items.
5. **Smart Email Management** – In Outlook, Copilot drafts responses, prioritizes emails, and summarizes lengthy conversations.
6. **Workflow Optimization** – Copilot automates repetitive tasks, enabling teams to focus on strategic initiatives.

How Microsoft Copilot Enhances Productivity for Leaders

For business leaders, productivity is more than just getting tasks done—it's about **maximizing efficiency, reducing cognitive load, and making informed decisions**. Microsoft Copilot serves as a force multiplier by handling time-consuming tasks, allowing executives to focus on high-value activities.

1. Enhancing Decision-Making with AI Insights

Leaders make critical decisions daily, often relying on vast amounts of data. Copilot assists by:

- Analyzing reports and summarizing key trends.
- Identifying patterns and anomalies in business data.
- Providing data-driven recommendations to optimize strategies.

Example: A CEO analyzing quarterly sales reports can use Copilot to extract key takeaways, identify market trends, and generate predictive insights for future planning.

2. Automating Administrative Tasks

Administrative tasks can consume valuable time. Copilot automates repetitive processes, such as:

- Scheduling meetings and suggesting optimal time slots.
- Drafting contracts and business proposals.

- Generating to-do lists and follow-ups.

Example: A manager preparing for a board meeting can use Copilot to summarize key financial reports, create PowerPoint slides, and draft agenda points—within minutes.

3. Boosting Communication Efficiency

Effective communication is at the heart of leadership. Copilot improves written and verbal communication by:

- Generating polished and professional emails.
- Suggesting responses based on previous conversations.
- Translating and summarizing long documents.

Example: A team leader in a multinational company can use Copilot to quickly translate reports, draft responses to clients, and summarize meeting minutes for global teams.

4. Improving Workflow Collaboration in Microsoft Teams

In today's remote and hybrid work environment, seamless collaboration is critical. Microsoft Copilot enhances teamwork by:

- Generating real-time meeting transcriptions and summaries.
- Highlighting key discussion points and action items.
- Providing contextual responses within Microsoft Teams chats.

Example: A project manager in a virtual team can use Copilot to summarize meetings, create action items, and track deadlines across multiple teams.

5. Transforming Data Analysis in Excel

Data-driven decision-making is essential for leaders. Copilot's capabilities in Excel revolutionize the way data is analyzed and interpreted:

- Predictive analytics – Forecast sales, trends, and business risks.
- Automated visualizations – Generate charts, graphs, and dashboards instantly.
- Data storytelling – Convert raw data into insightful business narratives.

Example: A CFO can use Copilot to quickly analyze company finances, generate budget projections, and identify cost-saving opportunities—without requiring advanced Excel skills.

Microsoft's AI Ecosystem: Transforming Workflows for Leaders

Beyond Copilot, Microsoft's AI ecosystem extends across Azure AI, Dynamics 365, and Power Platform, offering advanced AI-driven automation tools for businesses.

1. Azure AI: Enterprise-Grade AI Capabilities

Microsoft Azure provides cloud-based AI services that help businesses develop custom AI solutions, including:

- Computer Vision – AI-powered image recognition for quality control.
- Speech Recognition – Automated transcription for customer service.
- Machine Learning – Custom AI models for business insights.

Example: A logistics company uses Azure AI to predict supply chain disruptions and optimize delivery routes in real-time.

2. Dynamics 365: AI-Powered Business Intelligence

Microsoft Dynamics 365 integrates AI with customer relationship management (CRM) and enterprise resource planning (ERP), helping businesses:

- Automate customer interactions.
- Enhance sales forecasting.
- Improve operational efficiency.

Example: A sales director can use Dynamics 365 AI to predict customer needs, personalize marketing strategies, and optimize lead generation efforts.

3. Power Platform: AI-Driven Process Automation

Microsoft's Power Platform enables businesses to build AI-powered applications and automate workflows:

- Power Automate – Automates repetitive business tasks.
- Power BI – Provides AI-powered business analytics.
- Power Apps – Allows non-technical users to create AI-driven apps.

Example: A manufacturing company uses Power Automate to streamline inventory management, reducing waste and improving efficiency.

The Future of AI in Microsoft's Ecosystem

Microsoft continues to innovate, integrating AI into every aspect of business operations. The future of AI in Microsoft's ecosystem includes:

- Enhanced AI personalization – AI assistants that adapt to individual work styles.
- Real-time AI collaboration – AI-powered brainstorming and content generation.

- Advanced AI security – Protecting businesses from cyber threats using AI-driven defense mechanisms.

Microsoft Copilot and its AI ecosystem represent the next frontier in business automation and innovation. Leaders who adopt AI-powered tools will gain a competitive edge, enabling them to work smarter, drive efficiency, and foster continuous innovation.

AI is no longer a futuristic concept—it is here, transforming how businesses operate and how leaders make decisions. Microsoft Copilot is at the forefront of this transformation, offering powerful AI capabilities that enhance productivity, automate workflows, and drive innovation.

Leaders who embrace Copilot and Microsoft's AI ecosystem will be better equipped to navigate the complexities of the digital era, lead their teams effectively, and unlock new levels of business success.

PART 2: PRACTICAL APPLICATIONS OF AI IN LEADERSHIP

CHAPTER 4: UNLOCKING AI'S POTENTIAL IN EVERYDAY LEADERSHIP TASKS

AI is rapidly transforming the way leaders manage teams, make decisions, and drive innovation. What was once considered futuristic technology is now an essential tool for businesses, governments, and organizations worldwide. From strategic decision-making to automating repetitive tasks, AI empowers leaders to optimize operations, enhance efficiency, and stay ahead in an increasingly competitive landscape.

This chapter explores how AI can be leveraged in leadership roles, focusing on two key areas: using AI for smarter decision-making and automating routine tasks for maximum efficiency. Leaders who embrace AI not only gain a competitive edge but also create more agile, responsive, and innovative organizations.

AI in Strategic Decision-Making: From Insight to Action

In the fast-paced world of leadership, the ability to make informed, data-driven decisions is crucial. AI has transformed strategic decision-making by providing leaders with real-time insights, predictive analytics, and automated data processing. No longer do executives need to rely solely on intuition or time-consuming manual analysis—AI offers deep, actionable intelligence that enhances decision-making at every level.

The Role of AI in Decision-Making

AI supports leaders by:

- Processing vast amounts of data quickly and efficiently.

- Identifying patterns and trends that might be missed by human analysis.
- Predicting outcomes using historical data and machine learning.
- Providing real-time recommendations to guide strategic choices.

Instead of spending hours sifting through spreadsheets and reports, AI allows leaders to focus on interpreting insights and making high-impact decisions.

AI-Powered Predictive Analytics

Predictive analytics is one of AI's most powerful tools for leadership. By analyzing past and present data, AI can forecast future trends, enabling leaders to:

- Anticipate market shifts before they happen.
- Optimize supply chains based on demand predictions.
- Enhance customer experience by personalizing services.

Example: A retail CEO using AI-driven analytics can predict which products will be in high demand during different seasons, allowing for better inventory management and reduced waste.

AI in Risk Assessment and Mitigation

AI excels at identifying risks before they become problems. With machine learning algorithms, businesses can detect potential financial risks, cybersecurity threats, and operational inefficiencies.

Example: A financial institution can use AI to analyze transactions and flag unusual activities, preventing fraud before it occurs.

AI-driven dashboards and business intelligence tools provide leaders with up-to-the-minute insights, allowing for rapid and effective decision-making. These tools analyze real-time data from multiple sources, ensuring that leaders always have the most current and relevant information.

Example: A logistics manager can use AI-powered dashboards to track shipments in real time, rerouting deliveries based on weather conditions or traffic congestion.

Human-AI Collaboration in Leadership

While AI can process data and generate insights, the final decision-making still relies on human expertise. Leaders must:

- **Use AI as a support tool**, not a replacement for human judgment.
- **Interpret AI-driven insights** through the lens of industry knowledge.
- **Combine AI recommendations with ethical considerations** for balanced decision-making.

By leveraging AI effectively, leaders can make smarter, faster, and more strategic decisions that drive business success.

Automating Routine Tasks with AI for Maximum Efficiency

In leadership, time is a valuable resource. AI automation allows leaders to streamline repetitive, time-consuming tasks, freeing them up to focus on strategic priorities. From scheduling meetings to managing customer inquiries, AI-driven automation tools optimize workflows and enhance productivity.

The Power of AI Automation

AI-powered automation transforms leadership tasks by:

- **Eliminating manual processes**, reducing errors and inefficiencies.
- **Speeding up administrative workflows**, improving overall efficiency.
- **Allowing employees to focus on higher-value work**, boosting innovation and creativity.

AI in Administrative Task Management

Routine administrative tasks often consume significant time. AI tools now assist in:

- **Email management** – AI-powered assistants like Microsoft Copilot draft, summarize, and prioritize emails.
- **Meeting scheduling** – AI calendars suggest optimal meeting times and automate invites.
- **Document generation** – AI tools create reports, contracts, and summaries in seconds.

Example: A department head using AI scheduling assistants can instantly coordinate meeting times across multiple time zones without manual back-and-forth emails.

AI in Customer Support and Communications

AI chatbots and virtual assistants handle routine customer inquiries, reducing the workload for human employees while providing 24/7 service. These AI tools:

- Respond to FAQs, freeing up human agents for complex queries.
- Personalize interactions, improving customer satisfaction.
- Analyze sentiment to gauge customer emotions and concerns.

Example: A business owner implementing AI-driven chat support can reduce customer wait times and improve engagement without hiring additional staff.

AI in Financial and Data Management

AI-powered financial tools streamline accounting, budgeting, and data analysis by:

- Automating expense tracking and invoice processing.
- Providing real-time financial insights.
- Detecting anomalies in transactions to prevent fraud.

Example: A CFO using AI-powered accounting software can automatically generate reports, detect discrepancies, and ensure compliance with financial regulations.

AI in Workflow Optimization

AI tools help optimize business workflows by:

- Automating repetitive HR tasks, such as employee onboarding and payroll processing.
- Managing supply chains, predicting inventory needs, and reducing waste.
- Enhancing project management, tracking progress, and assigning tasks dynamically.

Example: A project manager using AI-powered workflow automation can allocate resources efficiently, ensuring that teams stay on track with minimal delays.

Balancing Automation with Human Oversight

While AI automation is a game-changer, leaders must ensure:

- Human oversight remains in critical processes.
- Employees are trained to work alongside AI tools.
- Ethical considerations are addressed in AI-driven decisions.

By integrating AI automation into daily operations, leaders can maximize efficiency, reduce workload, and create space for strategic innovation. AI is not just about replacing tasks—it's about empowering leaders and teams to achieve more with less effort.

CHAPTER 5: REAL-LIFE AI USE CASES – PRACTICAL APPLICATIONS FOR LEADERS

Artificial Intelligence (AI) is no longer just a futuristic concept—it is actively shaping the way businesses operate today. Leaders across industries are using AI to enhance customer engagement, streamline workflows, optimize resources, and make better financial decisions. But how exactly does this work in real life?

Imagine you're the CEO of a fast-growing online retail business. You want to improve customer experience, optimize your operations, and ensure that every dollar spent brings value to your company. How can AI help? This chapter will break down real-world applications of AI that leaders like you can use to stay ahead of the competition.

Enhancing Customer Engagement with AI-Powered Personalization

One of the most powerful ways AI is transforming business is through personalized customer experiences. Consumers today expect brands to understand their needs and offer tailored recommendations. AI makes this possible by analyzing vast amounts of customer data and predicting what people are most likely to buy, watch, or listen to.

Think about your experience with Netflix. Have you ever noticed that the platform always seems to know what movie or TV show you might enjoy next? That's because Netflix uses AI algorithms to track your viewing history, analyze similar users' preferences, and suggest content that aligns with your interests. The same technology powers Spotify's personalized music recommendations and Amazon's "Customers who bought this also bought" feature.

Now, imagine you run an e-commerce clothing store. Instead of showing every customer the same homepage, AI can analyze their past purchases, browsing history, and preferences to display items they are most likely to buy. If a customer frequently buys athletic wear, AI can show them the latest running shoes or gym apparel instead of formal suits. This targeted approach leads to higher conversion rates and increased sales.

AI-powered chatbots also play a huge role in customer engagement. Take Sephora, a global beauty retailer, as an example. They use an AI chatbot on their website and app to recommend beauty products based on customers' skin types and preferences. The chatbot can answer questions, provide tutorials, and even help customers find the perfect foundation shade—all without needing a human representative. This improves response times and enhances the overall customer experience.

Personalized email marketing is another AI-driven strategy. Instead of sending the same promotional email to every subscriber, AI analyzes each customer's behavior and tailors emails accordingly. For instance, if a customer frequently buys organic skincare products, the AI system will send them promotions for similar eco-friendly items rather than generic deals.

By using AI to personalize experiences, businesses can foster stronger relationships with customers, increase sales, and build long-term brand loyalty.

Streamlining Operations and Workflow with AI Tools

As a leader, your time is valuable, and every minute spent on repetitive tasks is a minute lost on strategic decision-making. AI helps businesses automate processes and optimize workflows, allowing teams to focus on high-impact activities.

Consider how project management platforms like Asana and Monday.com use AI to streamline team collaboration. These platforms can automatically assign tasks based on team members' workloads, suggest deadlines based on project complexity, and even flag potential roadblocks before they become major issues.

Imagine you're managing a construction project with multiple deadlines and stakeholders. Instead of manually tracking progress, AI can analyze real-time data, predict potential delays, and suggest solutions. If bad weather is expected, AI can alert you in advance and recommend rescheduling outdoor work, helping you avoid costly delays.

AI is also revolutionizing supply chain management. Walmart, for instance, uses AI to predict demand and optimize inventory. Rather than overstocking or running out of products, Walmart's AI system analyzes historical sales data, weather patterns, and shopping trends to ensure the right amount of stock is available at the right time. This prevents waste, reduces costs, and ensures customers always find what they need.

In logistics, companies like UPS rely on AI to optimize delivery routes. AI-powered route planning reduces fuel consumption, shortens delivery times, and improves efficiency. For instance, UPS's ORION system analyzes traffic patterns, weather conditions, and package drop-off locations to determine the most efficient delivery route. This has helped the company save millions in fuel costs while improving delivery speed.

For HR departments, AI-powered platforms like LinkedIn Recruiter and HireVue help streamline hiring processes. Instead of manually sifting through hundreds of resumes, AI scans job applications, identifies the most qualified candidates, and even conducts initial interview screenings using video analysis. This speeds up the hiring process and ensures businesses hire the best talent.

By integrating AI into operations, businesses can reduce inefficiencies, lower costs, and create a more productive work environment.

Using AI to Optimize Resource Management and Strategy

Effective leadership requires making smart decisions about how to allocate resources. Whether it's managing time, finances, or workforce efficiency, AI provides valuable insights to help leaders make data-driven decisions.

Take workforce scheduling as an example. Restaurants and retail stores need to balance customer demand with labor costs. AI-powered scheduling tools analyze historical sales data, foot traffic, and seasonal trends to determine the optimal number of employees needed at any given time. This ensures businesses are never understaffed during busy hours or overstaffed during slow periods.

In the energy sector, AI is being used to reduce electricity costs. Google's DeepMind AI helps manage energy consumption in Google data centers, predicting cooling needs and adjusting air conditioning accordingly. This has reduced Google's energy use by 40%, resulting in massive cost savings and a lower environmental impact.

For business strategy, AI-driven analytics tools help companies make better investment decisions. Financial institutions use AI to analyze market trends, assess risks, and predict the best times to buy or sell stocks. Hedge funds like Renaissance Technologies rely on AI-powered trading algorithms to make real-time investment decisions, maximizing returns while minimizing risks.

AI also helps businesses identify new market opportunities. Suppose you run a chain of coffee shops and want to expand into a new city. AI can analyze demographic data, local consumer preferences, and foot traffic patterns to determine the best locations for new stores. This reduces the risk of opening in an unprofitable area and increases the chances of success.

By leveraging AI in resource management, leaders can make smarter, data-driven decisions that maximize efficiency and profitability.

Applying AI for Financial and Market Analysis

The finance industry has been one of the biggest adopters of AI, using it to analyze vast amounts of data, detect fraud, and optimize investment strategies.

Think about the last time you made an online payment. AI-powered fraud detection systems are constantly monitoring transactions for unusual activity. If a bank detects a sudden large withdrawal from an unfamiliar location, AI can flag the transaction and temporarily freeze the account until it is verified. This has significantly reduced cases of credit card fraud and cybercrime.

AI is also revolutionizing financial forecasting. Platforms like Bloomberg Terminal use AI to analyze stock market trends, economic indicators, and news events to predict future market movements. Hedge funds use similar AI-driven strategies to make fast, data-backed trading decisions.

Small businesses can also benefit from AI-driven financial tools. Accounting platforms like Xero and QuickBooks use AI to automate bookkeeping, track expenses, and generate financial reports. Instead of spending hours on spreadsheets, business owners can rely on AI to manage their finances efficiently.

In marketing, AI helps businesses analyze consumer behavior and optimize advertising strategies. Facebook and Google use AI to analyze user data and deliver highly targeted ads. If you've ever noticed ads for products you recently searched for, that's AI at work, ensuring businesses reach the right audience at the right time.

By applying AI in financial analysis, businesses can minimize risks, improve decision-making, and increase profitability.

AI is no longer an optional tool—it is a necessity for leaders who want to stay competitive. From personalizing customer experiences to optimizing operations, managing resources, and analyzing financial markets, AI is transforming the way businesses operate.

Leaders who embrace AI will have a strategic advantage, allowing them to make smarter decisions, reduce inefficiencies, and drive business growth. The key is to stay informed, experiment with AI solutions, and integrate them effectively into daily operations.

As AI continues to evolve, businesses that adapt will be better positioned to thrive in the digital age. The future belongs to leaders who understand how to harness AI's full potential.

CHAPTER 6: AI FOR COMMUNICATION AND CONTENT CREATION

Effective communication is at the heart of leadership. Whether it's drafting emails, writing reports, delivering presentations, or creating content that positions you as a thought leader, the way you communicate can determine your influence and impact. AI is revolutionizing communication by making it faster, more efficient, and more engaging.

Imagine being able to draft a compelling business report in minutes, automate customer responses without losing a personal touch, or create high-quality content that attracts a global audience. That's the power of AI in communication and content creation. Let's explore how AI can help leaders communicate more effectively.

AI-Powered Writing, Emails, and Reports

Writing is an essential skill for leaders, but it's also time-consuming. AI writing tools like ChatGPT, Grammarly, and Jasper AI can help craft clear, concise, and persuasive messages in a fraction of the time.

For instance, if you're a manager who needs to send weekly performance reports to your team, AI can generate professional summaries based on key data points. Instead of spending hours writing reports, AI tools can analyze trends, highlight important insights, and structure your document in a polished format.

Emails are another area where AI can boost efficiency. Tools like Grammarly and Microsoft Copilot not only correct grammar and spelling but also suggest improvements in tone and clarity. If you struggle with writing diplomatic or persuasive emails, AI can help strike the right balance between professionalism and warmth.

Consider a busy executive who receives hundreds of emails daily. AI-powered email assistants like Superhuman or Google's Smart Compose can predict responses, prioritize important messages, and even draft replies. This allows leaders to focus on high-value interactions rather than getting lost in an overflowing inbox.

Meeting notes and transcriptions are also simplified with AI. Tools like Otter.ai and Fireflies automatically transcribe meetings and summarize key points, ensuring that no critical information is lost. This is especially helpful for leaders managing multiple teams or remote employees.

By integrating AI into writing, email management, and reporting, leaders can communicate more efficiently, reduce errors, and focus on strategic decision-making.

Enhancing Presentations and Public Speaking with AI Tools

Public speaking is a crucial skill for leaders, whether they're pitching ideas, delivering keynote speeches, or leading meetings. AI is now transforming how presentations are created and delivered.

PowerPoint and Google Slides have AI-powered features that help design visually appealing slides. Tools like Beautiful.ai and Canva's AI design assistant can format slides, suggest layouts, and even recommend visual elements to enhance engagement. Instead of spending hours tweaking a presentation, AI can handle the design while you focus on delivering a compelling message.

Speech improvement tools like Yoodli and Orai use AI to analyze speech patterns, tone, and pacing. If you're preparing for a major presentation, these tools provide feedback on your delivery, helping you refine your speaking style. They can detect filler words, suggest pauses, and ensure you maintain audience engagement.

AI-powered teleprompters, such as PromptSmart, can help speakers maintain eye contact while reading prepared scripts. Unlike traditional teleprompters, AI versions adjust scrolling speed based on your speech pace, ensuring a natural delivery.

For virtual meetings, tools like Zoom AI Companion can generate real-time captions and summaries, making presentations more accessible and easier to follow. If you're presenting to a global audience, AI can even provide real-time translations, breaking down language barriers.

By leveraging AI in presentations and public speaking, leaders can deliver more impactful messages, improve audience engagement, and boost their confidence as communicators.

Automating and Scaling Content for Thought Leadership

Thought leadership is about establishing yourself as an authority in your field. Whether you're writing articles, creating videos, or engaging on social media, AI can help you produce high-quality content at scale.

AI-powered content creation tools like Jasper, Writesonic, and Copy.ai generate blog posts, articles, and social media content based on given prompts. If you're a business leader who wants to share industry insights but struggles with writing, AI can help structure your thoughts into compelling narratives.

Video content is another major area where AI plays a role. Tools like Synthesia and Pictory use AI to create professional videos without the need for a film crew. Leaders can generate AI-powered avatars to deliver messages, create explainer videos, or even produce personalized customer outreach videos.

AI also assists with SEO (Search Engine Optimization), helping content rank higher on Google. Platforms like Clearscope and Surfer SEO analyze search trends and suggest keyword optimizations, ensuring that articles and blogs reach the right audience.

For social media engagement, AI tools like Buffer and Lately analyze past performance and recommend the best times to post, the most engaging content formats, and even auto-generate captions. This allows leaders to maintain an active presence without manually managing every post.

Consider an entrepreneur who wants to establish a strong LinkedIn presence but lacks the time to write daily updates. AI can generate topic ideas, draft engaging posts, and even suggest responses to comments, helping them build their personal brand effortlessly.

By automating content creation, AI enables leaders to share their expertise, build credibility, and expand their influence without investing excessive time.

AI is revolutionizing communication by making writing, presentations, and content creation faster, more efficient, and more impactful. Whether you're drafting reports, delivering speeches, or building a thought leadership platform, AI can help you communicate with clarity and confidence.

Leaders who embrace AI-powered communication tools will not only save time but also enhance their ability to connect with audiences, inspire teams, and establish themselves as industry experts. The key is to experiment with AI tools, integrate them into daily workflows, and refine strategies based on results.

As AI continues to evolve, the future of leadership communication will be defined by those who know how to harness its full potential.

CHAPTER 7: AI FOR DATA ANALYSIS AND BUSINESS INTELLIGENCE

In today's fast-paced business world, leaders can no longer rely solely on intuition or historical data to make decisions. The ability to analyze real-time information, predict market trends, and assess risks is crucial for staying ahead of the competition. AI-powered data analysis and business intelligence tools are transforming the way leaders interpret information, extract valuable insights, and make strategic choices with confidence.

This chapter explores how AI enhances data interpretation, market research, and decision-making, helping leaders gain a competitive edge in an increasingly data-driven economy.

Using AI to Interpret Business Metrics and Predict Trends

Businesses generate vast amounts of data daily—sales reports, customer interactions, website analytics, financial transactions, and more. Traditionally, leaders relied on spreadsheets and manual reports to interpret these metrics, which was time-consuming and prone to errors. AI has changed this by automating data analysis and providing real-time insights.

AI-driven analytics platforms, such as Tableau, Google Looker, and Microsoft Power BI, process large datasets within seconds, identifying patterns and trends that might otherwise go unnoticed. For example, an e-commerce company can use AI to track customer behavior, determine peak shopping hours, and predict which products will sell the most in the coming months.

Predictive analytics, powered by machine learning, allows businesses to forecast future trends with high accuracy. Financial institutions, for instance, use AI to anticipate stock market fluctuations, helping investors make informed decisions. Similarly, retail businesses can use AI to predict demand surges, ensuring they stock the right inventory ahead of time.

Case Study: Netflix's AI-Powered Recommendation System Netflix uses AI-driven predictive analytics to recommend content to users based on their viewing history. By analyzing past behavior, AI determines what a user is likely to watch next, enhancing customer satisfaction and increasing engagement. Business leaders can adopt similar AI models to anticipate customer needs and personalize experiences.

By leveraging AI in business metrics analysis, leaders can identify opportunities, optimize strategies, and stay ahead of market changes before they happen.

AI in Competitive Market Research and Risk Assessment

Understanding competitors and assessing risks are essential for strategic decision-making. AI has revolutionized market research by collecting and analyzing competitor data at scale. Instead of manually sifting through reports, leaders can use AI to track industry trends, monitor competitors' pricing strategies, and analyze customer sentiment in real-time.

AI tools like Crayon, Brandwatch, and SEMrush provide deep insights into competitors' digital marketing efforts, website traffic, and customer engagement strategies. For instance, a company launching a new product can use AI to analyze similar offerings in the market, understand pricing trends, and identify gaps that can be leveraged for differentiation.

Risk assessment is another area where AI shines. Financial institutions use AI-powered risk models to evaluate credit scores and detect potential fraud.

Similarly, supply chain leaders use AI to assess geopolitical risks, weather patterns, and logistical disruptions to minimize delays and ensure smooth operations.

Example: AI in Risk Management at JPMorgan JPMorgan Chase, one of the world's largest banks, uses AI to detect fraudulent transactions by analyzing spending patterns in real-time. Their AI-driven fraud detection system flags suspicious activities instantly, preventing financial losses and improving security. This same concept can be applied to other industries, such as cybersecurity, to identify potential threats before they escalate.

AI doesn't just analyze past data—it actively scans for risks, making it an essential tool for leaders who want to navigate uncertainties with confidence.

How AI Helps Leaders Make Smarter, Data-Driven Decisions

The true power of AI in business intelligence lies in its ability to turn raw data into actionable insights. AI-driven decision support systems help leaders weigh different scenarios, test hypotheses, and determine the best course of action.

For example, AI chatbots like ChatGPT or IBM Watson can act as virtual advisors, answering complex business questions based on real-time data. A CEO can ask, "What are the financial risks of expanding into a new market?" and receive an AI-generated report outlining potential challenges, competitor presence, and market demand.

AI-powered decision-making tools also enhance supply chain management. Companies like Amazon use AI to optimize delivery routes, reduce operational costs, and ensure faster shipping times. Leaders in logistics can use similar AI models to predict delivery delays, optimize inventory levels, and improve overall efficiency.

Case Study: AI-Driven Decision-Making at Coca-Cola Coca-Cola leverages AI-powered data analytics to optimize product development and marketing strategies. By analyzing social media conversations and customer feedback, AI helps the company identify emerging beverage trends and develop new flavors that resonate with consumers. This data-driven approach ensures that new products have a higher success rate in the market.

The ability to process and interpret data quickly gives leaders a competitive advantage, allowing them to act proactively rather than reactively. With AI, decision-making becomes not just faster, but also smarter and more strategic.

AI is reshaping how business leaders interpret data, conduct market research, assess risks, and make decisions. By using AI-powered analytics and predictive tools, leaders can anticipate trends, understand competitors, and optimize strategies with confidence.

Businesses that embrace AI-driven intelligence will not only reduce uncertainty but also gain a sharper competitive edge. In the future, AI will be an essential co-pilot for every decision-making process, helping leaders transform data into actionable business success.

CHAPTER 8: AI FOR PRODUCTIVITY AND TIME MANAGEMENT

In a world where leaders are constantly bombarded with meetings, emails, and decision-making, time is one of the most valuable resources. The ability to manage it effectively can determine whether a leader thrives or struggles under pressure. AI has become an indispensable tool for enhancing productivity, optimizing schedules, and reducing cognitive overload.

This chapter explores how AI-driven solutions can streamline time management, automate routine tasks, and serve as a virtual assistant, enabling leaders to focus on high-impact work.

AI-Driven Scheduling and Task Prioritization

One of the biggest challenges for leaders is managing their time efficiently. With countless meetings, project deadlines, and administrative tasks, it's easy to get overwhelmed. AI-driven scheduling tools can alleviate this burden by automating the process of organizing meetings, prioritizing tasks, and ensuring a well-structured workflow.

Smart assistants like Microsoft Copilot, Google's AI-powered calendar, and x.ai use machine learning to analyze your work habits, detect time conflicts, and suggest optimal meeting times. Instead of manually finding a slot for a meeting, AI can instantly check everyone's availability and schedule it at the best possible time.

For instance, imagine a CEO who needs to coordinate meetings across different time zones. AI scheduling tools automatically adjust time zones, suggest ideal meeting slots, and send calendar invites without requiring human intervention. This eliminates back-and-forth emails and streamlines time management.

Beyond scheduling, AI can also prioritize tasks based on urgency and importance. Tools like Motion and Todoist use AI to rank tasks based on deadlines, workload, and past behavior, ensuring that leaders tackle the most critical work first.

Example: AI-Powered Task Management at Google

Google's AI-powered task manager integrates with Gmail and Google Calendar to analyze incoming emails and automatically create action items. If a manager receives an email about a project update, AI can instantly add it as a task, set a reminder, and even suggest a time to address it based on the leader's schedule.

By leveraging AI for scheduling and task prioritization, leaders can free up mental energy for strategic decision-making rather than getting lost in administrative chaos.

Reducing Decision Fatigue with AI Assistance

Decision fatigue is a real challenge for leaders who make hundreds of decisions daily. From approving budgets to selecting candidates for key positions, constant decision-making can lead to mental exhaustion, resulting in poor choices. AI can significantly reduce decision fatigue by handling routine and repetitive decisions, allowing leaders to focus on critical matters.

AI-driven recommendation systems analyze data to provide well-informed suggestions, eliminating the need for leaders to start from scratch. For example, AI-powered email assistants can suggest responses based on previous interactions, reducing the time spent drafting emails.

In hiring, AI-driven applicant tracking systems (ATS) like Greenhouse and HireVue scan resumes, rank candidates based on qualifications, and suggest the best fits for a role. Instead of manually reviewing hundreds of applications, leaders can focus on interviewing the top candidates recommended by AI.

Case Study: AI in Decision-Making at Amazon

Amazon uses AI to automate supply chain decisions. The company's AI systems analyze customer demand, weather patterns, and shipping conditions to decide which warehouses should stock specific products. This eliminates the need for managers to manually calculate inventory needs, reducing decision fatigue while improving efficiency.

By offloading routine decisions to AI, leaders can preserve their cognitive resources for more strategic and creative thinking.

Delegating Smarter: AI as a Virtual Chief of Staff

In the past, executives relied on human assistants to manage their schedules, filter communications, and prepare reports. Today, AI can perform many of these tasks, acting as a virtual chief of staff that enhances leadership effectiveness.

AI-powered virtual assistants like ChatGPT, Google Assistant, and Microsoft Copilot can draft reports, summarize meetings, and even generate insights based on business data. These tools help leaders stay informed without getting bogged down in administrative tasks.

For instance, an AI-powered assistant can analyze a company's sales reports and provide a brief summary highlighting key trends. Instead of spending hours reviewing spreadsheets, a leader can quickly grasp the insights needed for decision-making.

Example: AI-Powered Executive Assistance at IBM

IBM's Watson Assistant helps executives manage their workflows by summarizing emails, setting priorities, and offering data-driven recommendations. It acts as a digital chief of staff, ensuring that leaders stay focused on high-impact tasks rather than administrative details.

With AI as a virtual chief of staff, leaders can streamline operations, reduce stress, and dedicate their time to innovation and strategic planning.

AI is transforming productivity and time management for leaders by automating scheduling, reducing decision fatigue, and acting as a virtual assistant. By embracing AI-driven tools, leaders can optimize their workdays, enhance efficiency, and focus on what truly matters—driving growth and innovation.

In the future, AI will not replace leadership but will amplify its effectiveness. Those who leverage AI for productivity will find themselves ahead of the curve, making smarter decisions with less effort and maximizing their time for what truly counts.

PART 3: INTEGRATING AI INTO YOUR ORGANIZATION

CHAPTER 9: A THREE-MONTH AI ADOPTION PLAN FOR LEADERS

Integrating AI into an organization is not an overnight process. It requires a structured approach that balances learning, experimentation, and strategic implementation. Leaders who take a phased approach can ensure smoother transitions, minimize resistance, and maximize AI's impact.

This chapter outlines a three-month AI adoption plan that will guide leaders from basic AI awareness to full integration, ensuring that AI becomes a valuable asset in daily operations and long-term business strategy.

Month 1: Getting Familiar with AI Tools and Applications

The first month is all about education, exploration, and building confidence with AI tools. Many leaders hesitate to adopt AI because they fear it is too complex or that it might replace human jobs. However, understanding AI's capabilities—and its limitations—will allow leaders to see it as an enabler rather than a threat.

Step 1: Assess Your Organization's AI Readiness

Before diving into AI implementation, leaders need to evaluate their organization's current digital maturity. Questions to consider include:

- What are the existing pain points in workflow efficiency, data management, or customer engagement?
- How tech-savvy is the workforce?
- What AI tools (if any) are already in use?

Conducting an internal AI assessment can reveal where AI can add the most value and where employees may need training.

Step 2: Explore AI Tools That Align with Leadership Needs

Leaders should spend time exploring AI-powered tools that can enhance productivity and decision-making. Some key AI tools to explore include:

- ChatGPT or Microsoft Copilot for drafting reports, summarizing meetings, and generating ideas
- Notion AI or ClickUp for automating project management
- Grammarly or Jasper AI for content generation and communication
- Tableau or Power BI for AI-driven data visualization

For example, a CEO struggling with email overload can start using AI email assistants that prioritize important messages and suggest quick replies.

Step 3: Educate the Team and Address AI Misconceptions

Leaders must ensure that their teams are comfortable with AI by offering AI awareness sessions. These sessions can help employees understand how AI enhances their work rather than replacing them.

Example: At a global consulting firm, leadership introduced AI through "AI Thursdays," where employees tested different AI tools and shared their experiences. This fostered a culture of learning and reduced fears about AI adoption.

By the end of Month 1, leaders and teams should have a foundational understanding of AI tools and their potential applications.

Month 2: Integrating AI into Daily Leadership Activities

With a solid AI foundation, the second month focuses on practical implementation. The goal is to start using AI tools in daily leadership tasks and measure their impact.

Step 1: Identify AI Use Cases in Leadership Workflows

Leaders should identify specific tasks where AI can provide immediate benefits. Common AI applications include:

- Automating repetitive tasks like scheduling meetings and responding to routine emails
- Enhancing decision-making through AI-driven business intelligence tools
- Improving communication with AI-generated reports and presentations

For instance, a marketing executive can use AI to analyze customer sentiment from social media and tailor campaigns accordingly.

Step 2: Assign AI Champions Within Teams

To ensure AI adoption is successful, organizations should designate "AI champions" within different departments. These individuals can test AI tools, provide feedback, and help others embrace AI.

Example: A retail company introduced AI-driven chatbots to handle customer service queries. The AI champion in the customer service team trained employees on how to collaborate with AI, reducing response times by 40%.

Step 3: Monitor AI's Effectiveness and Gather Feedback

Leaders should track AI's impact on productivity and efficiency. Simple performance indicators include:

- Time saved per task (e.g., AI scheduling tools reducing meeting coordination time)
- Error reduction in manual data analysis through AI automation
- Employee satisfaction and ease of use

Companies like PwC and Deloitte conduct AI adoption surveys every two weeks to adjust AI strategies based on employee feedback.

By the end of Month 2, AI should be an active part of leadership workflows, demonstrating measurable benefits.

Month 3: Positioning AI as a Strategic Partner for Long-Term Success

The final month focuses on embedding AI into the organization's long-term strategy. This means shifting AI from a mere tool to an essential business partner that drives innovation and growth.

Step 1: Develop an AI Roadmap for the Organization

Leaders should work with IT and strategy teams to map out a long-term AI adoption plan, considering:

- Scaling AI initiatives across different departments
- Investing in AI training programs for employees
- Integrating AI into customer experience strategies

Example: A logistics company implemented AI-powered demand forecasting to optimize inventory. After testing AI in one region, they expanded the solution company-wide, reducing inventory costs by 20%.

Step 2: Establish AI Ethics and Compliance Guidelines

As AI adoption grows, so do ethical concerns. Leaders must establish responsible AI use policies, covering:

- Data privacy and security
- Bias mitigation in AI decision-making
- Transparency in AI-generated insights

Example: Microsoft's AI ethics framework ensures that its AI models are fair, transparent, and aligned with ethical business practices. Leaders can adopt similar frameworks to maintain trust and compliance.

Step 3: Foster a Culture of Continuous AI Learning

AI is evolving rapidly. To stay ahead, leaders must create an environment where employees continuously learn about AI advancements. This can include:

- AI upskilling programs for employees
- Regular AI strategy reviews to update AI use cases
- Partnerships with AI vendors and industry experts to stay informed

Example: Salesforce invests heavily in AI training for its workforce through "AI academies," ensuring that employees are always equipped with the latest AI knowledge.

By the end of Month 3, AI should be fully integrated into the leadership approach, with a clear plan for long-term AI-driven growth.

AI adoption is a journey, not a one-time event. By following this structured three-month plan, leaders can move from AI exploration to full-scale implementation with minimal resistance. The key is to start small, scale strategically, and continuously optimize AI applications.

AI isn't just a tool—it's a leadership partner that enhances decision-making, streamlines operations, and fosters innovation. Leaders who embrace AI today will build organizations that are future-ready, agile, and ahead of the competition.

CHAPTER 10: BUILDING AN AI-READY TEAM – FOSTERING A CULTURE OF EXPERIMENTATION

As AI continues to revolutionize industries, leaders must ensure their teams are prepared to embrace and leverage these advancements. AI is not just about technology; it's about people. Organizations that cultivate an AI-friendly culture will outpace competitors by fostering innovation, efficiency, and adaptability. This chapter explores how leaders can build an AI-ready team by fostering curiosity, continuous learning, and strategic alignment.

Cultivating an AI-Friendly Mindset Among Employees

The first step in building an AI-ready team is fostering the right mindset. Many employees are hesitant about AI, fearing it will replace jobs or create complexity in their workflow. Leaders must address these concerns by positioning AI as a tool that enhances human capabilities rather than replacing them.

How to Shift Mindsets:

1. **Debunk AI Myths** – Many employees believe AI is only for tech experts or that it will automate all jobs. Leaders should hold informational sessions explaining how AI complements human work rather than replacing it.
2. **Showcase Practical Benefits** – Instead of discussing AI in abstract terms, demonstrate real-world applications. For example, show how AI chatbots reduce customer service workload, allowing employees to focus on higher-value tasks.

3. **Encourage a Growth Mindset** – Employees should see AI as an opportunity to upskill and enhance their roles. Leaders can promote this by rewarding curiosity and experimentation.

Example: A financial services firm introduced an "AI Challenge" where employees explored AI tools like ChatGPT for automating reports and emails. This hands-on experience made AI adoption less intimidating and more engaging.

Providing AI Learning Opportunities for Continuous Growth

AI is evolving rapidly, and staying ahead requires continuous learning. Organizations that invest in AI education ensure their workforce remains competitive and innovative.

Ways to Provide AI Learning Opportunities:

- AI Training Workshops: Partner with AI experts to run internal workshops on using AI tools relevant to different job functions.
- Microlearning Modules: Provide bite-sized AI learning content that employees can access on demand.
- AI Certifications and Courses: Encourage employees to take AI-related courses on platforms like Coursera, Udemy, and LinkedIn Learning.
- AI Mentorship Programs: Pair tech-savvy employees with those less experienced to facilitate peer learning.

Example: Amazon's AI upskilling initiative offers free AI courses to its workforce, helping employees integrate AI into their daily operations. As a result, the company has improved efficiency across departments.

Communicating the Strategic Value of AI to Your Team

To drive AI adoption, employees must understand how AI aligns with the organization's goals and benefits them personally. Leaders should clearly communicate AI's strategic value in a way that resonates with their team.

Effective Communication Strategies:

1. **Link AI to Business Success** – Explain how AI contributes to the company's growth, efficiency, and competitiveness. For example, "By using AI-driven analytics, we can predict market trends faster than competitors."
2. **Personalize AI Benefits for Employees** – Employees are more likely to embrace AI if they see how it makes their jobs easier. Highlight use cases specific to their roles, such as AI-generated reports for analysts or AI-powered scheduling tools for managers.
3. **Be Transparent About AI Integration** – Employees fear what they don't understand. Regularly update them on AI adoption plans, address concerns, and invite their input in AI-related decisions.

Example: At a leading healthcare provider, the CEO held monthly "AI Town Halls" where employees could ask questions and see AI success stories within the organization. This open dialogue increased trust and enthusiasm for AI adoption.

Building an AI-ready team requires more than just implementing technology—it demands a shift in mindset, ongoing education, and clear communication. Leaders who foster a culture of AI experimentation will unlock new levels of innovation and efficiency within their organizations. By helping employees see AI as an enabler rather than a disruptor, businesses can create a future-ready workforce that thrives in the AI era.

CHAPTER 11: HOW TO EVALUATE AND INVEST IN AI TECHNOLOGIES

Artificial Intelligence is reshaping industries, from healthcare and finance to retail and logistics. For leaders, integrating AI into an organization requires more than just purchasing new software—it demands a strategic approach that aligns with business goals, maximizes return on investment (ROI), and ensures long-term scalability. This chapter delves into how leaders can evaluate AI vendors, understand the financial implications of AI adoption, and create a sustainable AI implementation strategy that enhances operational efficiency and drives innovation.

Assessing AI Vendors and Choosing the Right Tools

Choosing the right AI tool is one of the most critical decisions leaders will make when investing in AI. With hundreds of AI solutions available, from chatbots and automation platforms to predictive analytics and machine learning models, selecting the wrong tool can lead to wasted resources, inefficiencies, and even security risks. Leaders need a structured framework to evaluate AI vendors effectively.

Key Factors to Consider When Choosing an AI Vendor

1. **Alignment with Business Goals**

AI should not be a gimmick—it must solve a real business problem. Leaders should start by identifying a specific challenge AI can address.

Example: A retail company struggling with abandoned shopping carts can explore AI-driven personalized recommendations and retargeting tools.

Example: A law firm drowning in legal documents can leverage AI-powered contract analysis software to speed up document review.

2. **Ease of Integration**

A good AI solution must fit seamlessly into existing workflows and IT infrastructure.

Example: A company using Microsoft 365 might prefer AI tools that integrate directly with Excel, Outlook, and Teams, such as Microsoft Copilot.

Example: A business heavily reliant on CRM (Customer Relationship Management) software like Salesforce should ensure AI-driven sales forecasting tools integrate smoothly.

3. **Data Security and Compliance**

AI systems handle vast amounts of sensitive data, from customer information to financial records. Leaders must ensure vendors follow strict data protection and compliance standards.

Example: Healthcare organizations must comply with HIPAA regulations when using AI for patient diagnostics or records management.

4. **Scalability**

AI solutions should grow with the business. Leaders should assess whether an AI tool can handle increasing data volumes and support evolving business needs.

Example: A startup using AI for customer support may need a tool that can transition from handling hundreds of queries per day to millions as the company scales.

5. **User-Friendliness and Employee Adoption**

Even the most advanced AI solution will fail if employees struggle to use it.

Example: A marketing team using AI-driven content generation should have access to an intuitive interface, training resources, and responsive customer support.

6. **Vendor Reputation and Customer Support**

Reliable customer support is crucial for troubleshooting and optimizing AI tools. Leaders should research vendors by reviewing case studies, testimonials, and customer feedback.

Example: A logistics company selecting an AI-powered route optimization tool should consider vendors with a proven track record in supply chain efficiency.

The Economics of AI Adoption: Costs vs. ROI

AI investments come with upfront costs, ongoing expenses, and long-term benefits. Leaders must analyze the financial impact before committing to AI adoption.

Understanding AI Costs

1. **Software and Licensing Fees**

Most AI tools operate on subscription-based pricing models, with costs varying based on features, number of users, and data processing capabilities.

Example: AI-powered customer service chatbots like ChatGPT Enterprise and IBM Watson have different pricing tiers depending on usage volume.

2. **Infrastructure and Cloud Computing**

Some AI applications require powerful computing resources, either on-premises or cloud-based.

Example: A company running AI-powered fraud detection on large transaction datasets may need scalable cloud solutions like AWS AI or Google Cloud AI.

3. Customization and Integration Costs

Off-the-shelf AI tools may require additional customization to align with an organization's specific needs.

Example: An insurance company using AI for claims processing may need to customize machine learning models to assess risk factors unique to their industry.

4. Training and Employee Upskilling

AI adoption requires employees to learn new tools and workflows. Training costs include workshops, online courses, and hiring AI specialists.

Example: A financial firm implementing AI-driven investment analysis tools may need to train advisors to interpret AI-generated insights.

5. Ongoing Maintenance and AI Model Updates

AI models require continuous optimization to stay relevant and effective.

Example: AI fraud detection tools must be updated regularly to recognize new scam patterns.

Measuring ROI from AI Investments

Leaders should measure AI's return on investment by evaluating tangible and intangible benefits.

1. **Efficiency Gains and Cost Savings**

AI automates repetitive tasks, reducing labor costs and allowing employees to focus on higher-value work.

Example: A legal firm using AI for contract analysis reduced document review time by 60%, saving thousands of billable hours.

2. **Revenue Growth and Sales Optimization**

AI-powered marketing and sales tools can boost conversions through personalized customer recommendations.

Example: E-commerce platforms like Amazon use AI to suggest products, increasing sales and customer satisfaction.

3. **Risk Reduction and Error Prevention**

AI minimizes human errors in critical business processes.

Example: A financial institution using AI for loan approvals reduced default rates by accurately predicting borrower risk.

4. **Customer Experience and Retention**

AI-driven personalization enhances user engagement and loyalty.

Example: Streaming platforms like Netflix use AI to recommend content, keeping users engaged longer.

Making AI Implementation Scalable and Sustainable

AI should not be a one-time experiment; it must be integrated into long-term business strategies.

1. **Start with Pilot Programs**

Rather than deploying AI across the entire organization, leaders should begin with small-scale pilot projects.

Example: A company implementing AI-driven customer support can start by automating FAQs before expanding AI to handle complex inquiries.

2. **Invest in AI Governance**

Organizations should establish AI policies covering ethics, accountability, and data privacy.

Example: A bank using AI for credit scoring must ensure transparency in decision-making to avoid biases.

3. **Ensure Human-AI Collaboration**

AI should enhance human capabilities, not replace employees.

Example: In healthcare, AI-powered diagnostic tools assist doctors in analyzing medical scans but do not replace their expertise.

4. **Regular Performance Monitoring and Optimization**
Leaders must track AI performance metrics and continuously refine models to maximize effectiveness.

- **Example:** AI-driven demand forecasting tools should be updated regularly to account for seasonal trends and market fluctuations.

AI is a transformative technology, but successful adoption requires strategic planning, careful vendor selection, and ongoing evaluation. Leaders must approach AI investments with a clear understanding of business objectives, financial considerations, and long-term scalability. By making informed decisions, businesses can unlock AI's full potential, driving efficiency, innovation, and competitive advantage in their industry.

CHAPTER 12: OVERCOMING COMMON AI CHALLENGES IN LEADERSHIP

Artificial Intelligence offers incredible opportunities for businesses, from automating tasks to enhancing decision-making. However, leaders must also be prepared to face challenges when implementing AI. Resistance from employees, ethical dilemmas, and the risk of AI failures can all hinder progress. This chapter explores practical strategies for overcoming these challenges, ensuring AI is integrated effectively while maintaining human oversight and control.

Managing Resistance to AI in the Workplace

AI adoption is not just a technical challenge—it is a cultural one. Employees often resist AI because they fear job loss, struggle to adapt to new technologies, or distrust automated decision-making. Leaders must proactively address these concerns to foster an AI-friendly workplace.

Why Employees Resist AI

1. **Job Security Fears:** Many employees worry that AI will replace their roles, making them obsolete.
2. **Lack of Understanding:** Employees unfamiliar with AI may view it as complex, intimidating, or unnecessary.
3. **Trust Issues:** Some people believe AI-driven decisions are unreliable, biased, or lack human empathy.
4. **Disruption to Routine:** Workers who have done things a certain way for years may resist changing their workflow.

1. **Educate and Communicate AI's Purpose**

Employees need to understand that AI is a tool to enhance their work, not replace them. Leaders should communicate how AI will help automate repetitive tasks, allowing employees to focus on more meaningful work.

o **Example:** A marketing team worried about AI-generated content should learn how AI can assist with brainstorming and analytics while still requiring human creativity.

2. **Involve Employees in the AI Adoption Process**

Workers should be included in discussions about AI implementation. When employees feel heard, they are more likely to support change.

o **Example:** A logistics company rolling out AI-powered inventory management can ask warehouse staff for feedback before finalizing deployment.

3. **Provide AI Training and Upskilling Programs**

Many employees fear AI because they lack the skills to work with it. Training programs can help them transition into AI-assisted roles.

o **Example:** Banks introducing AI-driven fraud detection should train staff to interpret AI-generated reports instead of manually analyzing transactions.

4. **Reframe AI as a Partner, Not a Replacement**

AI should be seen as an assistant that improves efficiency rather than a tool that eliminates jobs.

o **Example:** In healthcare, AI can assist doctors by analyzing X-rays quickly, but the final diagnosis still requires human expertise.

Avoiding AI Overdependence and Maintaining Human Oversight

While AI is powerful, overreliance on automated systems can lead to unintended consequences. Leaders must strike a balance between leveraging AI's capabilities and ensuring human judgment remains at the core of decision-making.

Risks of AI Overdependence

1. **Loss of Critical Thinking:** Relying too much on AI-generated insights can lead to leaders accepting results without questioning their accuracy.
2. **Ethical Blind Spots:** AI lacks human morality and can make decisions that may be legally or ethically questionable.
3. **Algorithmic Bias:** AI models learn from historical data, which may contain biases that lead to unfair outcomes.
4. **Technical Failures:** AI is not infallible—bugs, incorrect data inputs, or cybersecurity breaches can result in costly mistakes.

How to Ensure AI Remains a Support Tool, Not the Decision-Maker

1. **Maintain a "Human-in-the-Loop" Approach**

Leaders should ensure AI recommendations are reviewed and verified by human decision-makers.

   o **Example:** AI-powered hiring tools can help screen job applicants, but final hiring decisions should still involve HR professionals.
2. **Set AI Override Mechanisms**

AI should never have the final say in critical areas like finance, healthcare, or law.

- o **Example:** Self-driving cars use AI for navigation, but human drivers should have the ability to take control in emergencies.
   3. **Encourage Human Intuition and Expertise**

AI can process vast amounts of data, but it lacks intuition, creativity, and emotional intelligence.

- o **Example:** AI can suggest investment strategies, but financial advisors should consider economic trends and market psychology before making final decisions.
   4. **Regularly Audit AI Systems for Bias and Errors**

AI should be periodically reviewed to ensure it is making fair and accurate predictions.

- o **Example:** AI loan approval systems should be checked for racial or gender bias in lending decisions.

Navigating AI Failures and Unexpected Outcomes

Even the most sophisticated AI systems can fail, sometimes with serious consequences. Leaders must be prepared for AI malfunctions, misinterpretations, or unintended behaviors.

Common AI Failures

1. **Data Input Errors:** AI models depend on high-quality data; incorrect inputs can lead to faulty predictions.
   - o **Example:** A hospital using AI for diagnosing illnesses could receive incorrect results if patient data is entered incorrectly.
2. **AI Misinterpretation of Context:** AI lacks human reasoning and can make bizarre or harmful decisions based on patterns in data.
   - o **Example:** A chatbot trained on internet conversations started generating offensive responses because it learned from biased data.

3. **System Glitches and Cybersecurity Threats:** AI systems can be hacked or malfunction, causing data breaches or operational disruptions.
   - **Example:** An AI-powered trading system once caused a stock market flash crash by executing trades too rapidly based on incorrect signals.
4. **Overfitting and Inflexibility:** AI models can become too reliant on past data, making them ineffective in new or unexpected situations.
   - **Example:** AI-powered demand forecasting tools trained on pre-pandemic shopping habits struggled to adapt when COVID-19 changed consumer behavior overnight.

How Leaders Can Prepare for AI Failures

1. **Develop Contingency Plans**

Organizations should have backup plans if AI tools fail.

   - **Example:** A customer service department using AI chatbots should have human agents ready to take over in case of system outages.
2. **Implement AI Testing and Monitoring Protocols**

Regular testing can identify potential AI weaknesses before they cause harm.

   - **Example:** Financial institutions using AI for fraud detection should run test cases to ensure the system flags suspicious transactions accurately.
3. **Create Ethical AI Guidelines**

Businesses should establish ethical policies for AI usage, ensuring fair and responsible decision-making.

   - **Example:** AI hiring tools should be programmed to avoid discrimination based on race, gender, or age.
   -

4. **Encourage a Culture of AI Transparency**

Employees should feel comfortable questioning AI decisions rather than blindly accepting them.

- o **Example:** Doctors using AI for medical diagnoses should always have the final say on patient treatments.

AI adoption comes with challenges, but with the right leadership approach, these obstacles can be effectively managed. By addressing employee concerns, maintaining human oversight, and preparing for AI failures, leaders can build a workplace where AI is a valuable tool rather than a disruptive force. The key is to treat AI as a strategic partner—one that enhances human capabilities rather than replacing them.

PART 4: AI ETHICS, SECURITY, AND THE FUTURE OF LEADERSHIP

CHAPTER 13: SAFEGUARDING DATA AND ENSURING PRIVACY IN THE AI ERA

Data is the lifeblood of AI. Every interaction, every decision, every prediction AI makes is fueled by the data it ingests. While AI offers transformative potential—unlocking efficiencies, personalizing experiences, and predicting trends—it also introduces new vulnerabilities. The same data that powers innovation can, if misused or inadequately protected, expose businesses to cyber threats, regulatory fines, and reputational damage.

As a leader, you are responsible for ensuring that AI-driven data practices align with ethical standards, legal requirements, and security best practices. This chapter explores the risks and rewards of AI in data handling, outlines strategies to protect sensitive information, and provides a framework for evaluating AI vendors based on their commitment to privacy and security.

AI and Data Handling: A Double-Edged Sword

AI thrives on data—customer interactions, financial records, behavioral analytics, medical histories, and more. But with great power comes great responsibility. Mishandling data can erode trust, violate privacy laws, and expose organizations to cyber threats. Let's examine both the advantages and the challenges of AI-driven data handling.

The Benefits of AI-Driven Data Management

1. **Data-Driven Decision-Making:** AI can process and analyze massive datasets in real time, uncovering insights that would take human analysts weeks or months to identify.

- *Example:* AI-powered analytics platforms help businesses detect market trends, optimize supply chains, and predict customer behavior with remarkable accuracy.

2. **Process Automation and Efficiency Gains:** AI streamlines workflows by automating repetitive data-intensive tasks.
   - *Example:* AI can scan and categorize millions of emails, flagging phishing attempts and prioritizing urgent communications.

3. **Enhanced Cybersecurity Measures:** AI can detect anomalies in real-time, flagging suspicious activities before they escalate into full-blown security breaches.
   - *Example:* Banks use AI to monitor transactions and detect fraudulent activity based on unusual spending patterns.

4. **Personalized User Experiences:** AI can analyze customer preferences and behavior to deliver hyper-personalized recommendations.
   - *Example:* E-commerce platforms like Amazon use AI to suggest products based on browsing history, increasing customer engagement.

5. **Fraud Prevention and Risk Mitigation:** AI models can spot irregularities and potential fraud by analyzing data patterns across vast networks.
   - *Example:* Credit card companies use AI to flag unauthorized transactions and prevent financial fraud.

The Risks of AI in Data Handling

1. **Cybersecurity Threats and Data Breaches:** AI systems store and process vast amounts of sensitive information, making them prime targets for hackers.
   - *Example:* A cyberattack on an AI-powered healthcare system could expose millions of patient records.

2. **Privacy Concerns and Ethical Dilemmas:** AI's ability to collect and analyze personal data raises concerns about surveillance, consent, and data misuse.

- o *Example:* AI-driven facial recognition technology has been criticized for its potential to violate individual privacy.
3. **Bias and Discrimination:** AI models trained on biased data can unintentionally reinforce societal inequalities.
   - o *Example:* An AI-powered hiring tool that favors candidates from specific demographics can perpetuate workplace discrimination.
4. **Regulatory Compliance Challenges:** Global data protection laws such as GDPR (Europe) and CCPA (California) impose strict requirements on how companies collect, store, and use data.
   - o *Example:* Companies that fail to comply with GDPR can face fines of up to €20 million or 4% of global revenue.
5. **Lack of Transparency in AI Decision-Making:** Many AI models operate as "black boxes," making it difficult to understand how they reach decisions.
   - o *Example:* A customer denied a loan by an AI-powered system may not receive a clear explanation for the rejection.

Best Practices for Data Protection in AI Systems

Protecting data in AI systems requires a proactive, multi-layered approach. Here are some key strategies to safeguard sensitive information:

1. Encrypt Data at Every Stage

Encryption ensures that data remains secure even if intercepted. Organizations should encrypt data at rest (stored data) and in transit (data being transferred between systems).

- *Example:* Financial institutions encrypt credit card transactions to prevent cybercriminals from accessing sensitive banking details.

2. Anonymize and Mask Sensitive Data

Anonymization removes personally identifiable information (PII) before data is processed by AI models, reducing privacy risks.

- *Example:* Hospitals anonymize patient records to train AI models for disease diagnosis while protecting patient identities.

3. Implement Strict Access Controls

Not all employees need access to all data. Organizations should use role-based access controls (RBAC) to restrict data access based on job functions.

- *Example:* A marketing analyst may need access to customer demographics but not their financial records.

4. Conduct Regular AI Security Audits

Periodic security assessments help organizations identify vulnerabilities in AI systems and address potential threats before they lead to breaches.

- *Example:* A retail company using AI-powered recommendation engines should regularly audit its data sources to prevent unintended data leaks.

5. Ensure Transparency in AI Decision-Making

AI models should be designed to provide clear explanations for their decisions, fostering trust among users.

- *Example:* If an AI-driven recruitment tool rejects a candidate, it should provide a rationale based on specific qualifications and skills.

6. Adhere to Global Data Protection Regulations

Companies operating internationally must comply with varying privacy laws and standards.

- *Example:* A tech startup expanding to Europe must align its data policies with GDPR requirements to avoid legal repercussions.

How to Evaluate AI Vendors for Privacy and Security Compliance

When selecting an AI vendor, due diligence is essential. Here's a framework for assessing AI vendors based on their commitment to data privacy and security.

1. Verify Compliance with Industry Regulations

Ensure the vendor follows established data protection frameworks such as GDPR, CCPA, HIPAA (for healthcare), and ISO 27001 (for information security).

- *Example:* A financial firm should only partner with AI vendors that comply with strict financial data regulations.

2. Assess Data Security Measures

Ask about encryption protocols, multi-factor authentication, and data breach response strategies.

- *Example:* If an AI vendor does not offer end-to-end encryption, it may not be a reliable partner for handling sensitive data.

3. Demand Transparency in AI Algorithms

Avoid vendors that offer "black box" AI solutions with no visibility into how decisions are made.

- *Example:* A legal firm using AI for case predictions should select a platform that provides explainable AI insights.

4. Review Data Retention and Deletion Policies

Ensure vendors have clear policies for storing and deleting data, minimizing unnecessary risk.

- *Example:* A healthcare provider using AI for medical imaging should confirm that the vendor deletes old scans after a certain period.

5. Check for a Strong Cybersecurity Track Record

Investigate whether the vendor has experienced past security breaches and how they handled them.

- *Example:* A cloud-based AI provider with multiple security incidents may indicate poor security practices.

6. Evaluate Their Approach to Bias and Ethical AI Use

Ask vendors how they mitigate bias in their AI models to ensure fair outcomes.

- *Example:* An AI-driven credit scoring system should be tested for fairness across different demographic groups.

Leading with Accountability

As AI becomes increasingly embedded in business operations, leaders must prioritize data privacy and security. Safeguarding data isn't just about compliance—it's about trust. Employees, customers, and stakeholders must feel confident that their information is protected and used ethically.

By implementing best practices and rigorously evaluating AI vendors, organizations can harness the power of AI while minimizing risks. In the AI-driven future, those who manage data responsibly will not only avoid legal pitfalls but also build stronger, more resilient businesses.

CHAPTER 14: ETHICAL LEADERSHIP IN THE AGE OF AI

The integration of artificial intelligence into businesses and organizations presents a paradox: while AI has the potential to drive efficiency, innovation, and profitability, it also introduces profound ethical dilemmas. AI-powered systems influence hiring decisions, loan approvals, law enforcement practices, healthcare diagnoses, and even judicial rulings. If not carefully managed, AI can reinforce bias, create unfair advantages, and erode public trust.

Ethical leadership in the AI era requires a commitment to fairness, transparency, and accountability. Leaders must ensure that AI technologies are deployed in ways that benefit society while minimizing harm. In this chapter, we'll explore how to identify and address ethical challenges, mitigate bias, and foster responsible AI governance.

Addressing Ethical Challenges in AI Use

Ethical dilemmas in AI often arise when technology is applied without proper oversight or consideration of long-term consequences. Below are key challenges leaders must confront:

1. The Accountability Problem: Who is Responsible for AI Decisions?

When AI systems make mistakes—such as denying a qualified candidate a job or misdiagnosing a patient—who bears responsibility?

- Leaders must establish clear accountability frameworks, ensuring that AI-driven decisions remain subject to human oversight.
- *Example:* If an AI-driven hiring tool discriminates against certain applicants, HR and leadership must intervene to correct the bias rather than blame the technology.

2. The Trade-Off Between Innovation and Privacy

AI thrives on data, but excessive data collection can violate privacy rights. Striking a balance is crucial.

- Leaders should implement data minimization strategies—collecting only the data necessary for AI functions.
- *Example:* Retailers using AI to personalize customer experiences must ensure that consumer data is used responsibly and with consent.

3. The Risk of Mass Surveillance and Misuse of AI

AI-powered surveillance tools raise serious ethical concerns, particularly in law enforcement and public monitoring.

- Organizations must weigh security benefits against potential violations of civil liberties.
- *Example:* While facial recognition can enhance security at airports, its use by governments for mass surveillance has raised global concerns.

4. Job Displacement and Workforce Ethics

AI-driven automation is reshaping industries, often at the expense of human jobs.

- Ethical AI leadership requires retraining and upskilling workers, ensuring that AI enhances human work rather than replaces it.
- *Example:* Companies implementing AI chatbots should invest in employee reskilling programs rather than resorting to mass layoffs.

Navigating the Risks of Bias and Discrimination in AI Systems

One of AI's most significant challenges is bias—the tendency of algorithms to reflect and reinforce societal prejudices. Bias can creep into AI models through biased training data, flawed assumptions, or unintentional design errors.

1. Understanding How AI Bias Occurs

Bias in AI often stems from:

- **Historical Data Bias:** AI learns from past data, which may reflect societal inequalities.
- **Sampling Bias:** If an AI model is trained on non-representative data, it will yield skewed results.
- **Algorithmic Bias:** Developers' assumptions may unintentionally influence AI decision-making.

2. Strategies for Mitigating AI Bias

Leaders must actively work to minimize bias in AI systems by:

- **Ensuring Diverse and Representative Data:** AI should be trained on datasets that reflect all demographic groups.
- **Regularly Auditing AI Models:** AI systems should be tested for biased outputs and adjusted accordingly.
- **Building Explainable AI:** AI models should provide clear reasoning for their decisions, allowing for human review.

Example: A bank using AI for loan approvals must regularly audit its system to ensure it doesn't disproportionately deny loans to minority applicants.

Ensuring Fair and Transparent AI Decision-Making

Transparency is critical in AI ethics. People affected by AI decisions—employees, customers, and stakeholders—should understand how these decisions are made.

1. Explainable AI (XAI): Making AI Decisions Understandable

AI systems should not function as "black boxes." Instead, they must provide clear explanations for their outputs.

- *Example:* AI-driven credit scoring models should disclose why a customer was denied a loan.

2. AI Governance and Ethical Review Boards

Organizations should establish internal AI ethics committees to evaluate and approve AI deployments.

- *Example:* A healthcare institution using AI for patient diagnostics should have an oversight board ensuring ethical compliance.

By prioritizing ethical leadership, businesses can harness AI's power while safeguarding fairness, accountability, and public trust.

CHAPTER 15: CRAFTING A LONG-TERM AI STRATEGY FOR SUSTAINABLE GROWTH

AI is not just a short-term competitive advantage—it is a long-term strategic asset. However, to drive sustainable growth, organizations must develop a forward-thinking AI strategy that aligns with business objectives, measures impact effectively, and adapts to evolving technological landscapes.

Aligning AI Strategies with Business Objectives

AI adoption should not be a standalone initiative—it must be seamlessly integrated into an organization's broader goals. Leaders must ask: How can AI enhance efficiency, innovation, and customer satisfaction?

1. Identifying Core Areas Where AI Can Drive Value

AI can be applied across various business functions, such as:

- **Customer Service:** AI chatbots and virtual assistants improve response times and user experiences.
- **Operations and Supply Chain:** AI-driven demand forecasting optimizes inventory management.
- **Marketing and Sales:** AI-powered analytics provide personalized recommendations and targeted advertising.

2. Aligning AI Investments with Business Goals

- If a company prioritizes customer retention, AI should focus on personalization and predictive analytics.
- If operational efficiency is the goal, AI should be used to automate repetitive tasks and optimize workflows.

Example: A logistics company aiming to reduce delivery times should invest in AI-powered route optimization.

Setting and Measuring AI-Driven Goals for Organizational Impact

AI initiatives must be measurable to assess their effectiveness. Leaders should establish key performance indicators (KPIs) that track AI's impact on revenue, efficiency, and customer satisfaction.

1. Defining Key AI Performance Metrics

- **Efficiency Metrics:** Reduction in manual labor, processing times, or operational costs.
- **Revenue Metrics:** Increase in sales, customer retention, or conversion rates due to AI-driven insights.
- **Customer Experience Metrics:** Improvements in customer satisfaction scores or engagement rates.

Example: An e-commerce company should track AI's impact on product recommendation accuracy and resulting sales conversions.

2. Continuously Optimizing AI Models

AI systems require ongoing refinement. Organizations must:

- **Monitor AI performance in real-time.**
- **Collect user feedback and make necessary adjustments.**
- **Retrain AI models periodically to ensure accuracy and fairness.**

Adapting Your AI Strategy for Future Challenges and Opportunities

AI is evolving rapidly. Organizations that fail to adapt risk obsolescence. Leaders must anticipate industry shifts and continuously refine their AI strategies.

1. Preparing for Emerging AI Technologies

Organizations should stay ahead of trends such as:

- **Edge AI:** AI processing at the device level, reducing reliance on cloud computing.
- **AI-Powered Cybersecurity:** AI models that predict and prevent cyber threats.
- **Natural Language Processing (NLP):** More sophisticated AI-driven customer interactions.

2. Cultivating an AI-Ready Workforce

As AI reshapes job roles, organizations must:

- Invest in AI training for employees.
- Encourage cross-functional collaboration between AI experts and business leaders.
- Foster a culture of continuous learning to stay ahead of technological advancements.

3. Building an AI Governance Framework for the Future

- AI policies should evolve with changing regulations.
- Organizations should participate in ethical AI discussions and advocate for responsible AI use.

- Transparency and fairness should remain core principles of AI strategy.

By crafting a long-term AI strategy that is adaptable, measurable, and aligned with business objectives, organizations can ensure AI remains a driver of sustainable growth rather than a short-lived trend.

Leading AI into the Future

AI is not just a tool—it is a paradigm shift in how businesses operate. Ethical leadership, transparency, and strategic foresight will determine which organizations thrive in the AI era. Leaders who navigate AI's challenges responsibly will build companies that are not only technologically advanced but also resilient, ethical, and sustainable for the future.

CHAPTER 16: FUTURE-PROOFING YOUR LEADERSHIP—PREPARING FOR WHAT'S NEXT

The AI revolution is accelerating at an unprecedented pace, reshaping industries, economies, and the very nature of leadership. To stay ahead, leaders must adopt a future-proof mindset—one that embraces continuous learning, anticipates emerging trends, and evolves alongside technological advancements. In this chapter, we will explore how to prepare for new AI-driven leadership roles, identify and adapt to shifting AI trends, and cultivate a growth-oriented approach to leading in the AI age.

Preparing for Emerging AI Roles in Leadership

The traditional leadership landscape is shifting. As AI becomes embedded in business operations, new leadership roles are emerging, requiring a unique blend of technological fluency, ethical decision-making, and strategic foresight.

1. The Rise of AI-Focused Leadership Roles

Organizations are increasingly recognizing the need for specialized leadership positions dedicated to AI strategy and governance. Some of the emerging roles include:

- **Chief AI Officer (CAIO):** Oversees AI adoption, ethical considerations, and strategic alignment.
- **AI Ethics Officer:** Ensures AI systems comply with regulatory and moral standards.
- **Data and AI Governance Lead:** Manages AI transparency, accountability, and risk mitigation.

2. Skills Leaders Must Develop to Thrive in AI-Driven Roles

To remain relevant in the AI-powered future, leaders must cultivate skills that bridge the gap between technology and business strategy. Key competencies include:

- **AI Literacy:** Understanding AI capabilities, limitations, and implications for decision-making.
- **Data-Driven Decision-Making:** Leveraging AI insights to inform business strategies.
- **Change Management:** Guiding teams through digital transformation with adaptability and resilience.
- **Ethical AI Governance:** Ensuring fairness, transparency, and accountability in AI deployments.

Example: A CEO looking to future-proof their organization should invest in AI upskilling programs, ensuring that executives and teams can make informed AI-driven decisions.

Identifying and Adapting to New AI Trends in the Business World

AI is not a static technology—it continuously evolves. Future-ready leaders must monitor trends, anticipate disruptions, and proactively integrate AI advancements into their strategies.

1. Key AI Trends Shaping the Future of Leadership

- **Hyper-Personalization with AI:** AI-driven customer experiences will become more tailored, requiring leaders to rethink marketing and engagement strategies.
- **AI-Augmented Decision-Making:** AI will increasingly assist executives in making complex business choices based on predictive analytics.

- **Automation of Managerial Tasks:** AI will handle administrative functions like performance tracking and reporting, freeing leaders to focus on strategy and innovation.
- **AI-Powered Creativity:** AI tools will collaborate with humans to enhance creativity in content creation, design, and innovation.

2. How Leaders Can Stay Ahead of AI Trends

- **Continuous Learning:** Engage in AI courses, attend industry conferences, and participate in AI-focused leadership networks.
- **Cross-Industry Observations:** AI adoption in different industries can offer insights into potential applications in your field.
- **Experimentation and Pilot Programs:** Test AI applications within your organization before full-scale implementation.

Example: A retail executive staying ahead of AI trends might explore AI-driven inventory forecasting to optimize supply chain efficiency.

Developing a Growth Mindset to Lead in the AI Evolution

The leaders who thrive in the AI era will be those who embrace a **growth mindset**—the belief that skills, intelligence, and capabilities can be developed through effort, learning, and adaptation.

1. Shifting from AI Skepticism to AI Empowerment

Many leaders resist AI due to fear of change or uncertainty about its impact. However, forward-thinking leaders:

- View AI as an **enhancer** rather than a **replacement** for human decision-making.
- Emphasize **AI-human collaboration** to drive innovation and efficiency.

- Foster **a culture of experimentation**, where employees are encouraged to explore AI-driven improvements.

2. Encouraging an AI Learning Culture in Organizations

To future-proof leadership, organizations must create a culture that embraces AI literacy and continuous development. Steps include:

- **Providing AI Training:** Equip teams with the knowledge to leverage AI effectively.
- **Encouraging Cross-Disciplinary Collaboration:** AI solutions require input from multiple departments, not just IT.
- **Creating Safe Experimentation Spaces:** Allow teams to test AI solutions in controlled environments before full deployment.

Example: A forward-thinking business leader might implement internal AI workshops to ensure employees at all levels feel comfortable working with AI-powered tools.

GLOSSARY

- **Artificial Intelligence (AI)** – The simulation of human intelligence in machines, enabling them to learn, reason, and make decisions.
- **Algorithm** – A set of rules or instructions used by AI systems to process data and generate outputs.
- **Bias in AI** – The presence of prejudiced outcomes in AI models due to flawed training data or programming, leading to unfair or discriminatory results.
- **Chatbot** – An AI-powered software that simulates human conversation to assist with customer service, information retrieval, and other tasks.
- **Data-Driven Decision-Making** – The process of using AI to analyze data and derive insights that guide strategic business decisions.
- **Deep Learning** – A subset of machine learning that mimics the workings of the human brain using artificial neural networks to process large amounts of data.
- **Ethical AI** – The practice of developing and using AI systems in a way that is fair, transparent, and accountable, minimizing bias and ensuring responsible use.
- **Generative AI** – A type of AI that creates new content, such as text, images, and music, based on patterns learned from existing data.
- **Large Language Models (LLMs)** – AI models trained on vast amounts of text data to generate human-like language, such as ChatGPT.
- **Machine Learning (ML)** – A subset of AI that enables machines to learn from data and improve their performance without explicit programming.
- **Natural Language Processing (NLP)** – The branch of AI that focuses on enabling machines to understand, interpret, and generate human language.
- **Neural Networks** – AI models designed to function like the human brain, processing information through interconnected layers to identify patterns and make predictions.

- **Predictive Analytics** – The use of AI to analyze past data and forecast future trends, helping businesses anticipate market changes and consumer behavior.
- **Supervised Learning** – A machine learning approach where AI models are trained using labeled data, learning patterns from predefined inputs and outputs.
- **Unsupervised Learning** – A machine learning method where AI models analyze and categorize data without predefined labels, identifying patterns independently.

REFERENCES

1. Brynjolfsson, E. And McAfee, A. (2017) Machine, platform, crowd: Harnessing our digital future. New York: W.W. Norton & Company.
2. Daugherty, P.R. and Wilson, H.J. (2018) Human + Machine: Reimagining work in the age of AI. Boston: Harvard Business Review Press.
3. Russell, S. And Norvig, P. (2021) Artificial intelligence: A modern approach. 4th edn. Hoboken, NJ: Pearson.
4. Ng, A. (2018) AI transformation playbook: How to lead your company into the AI era. Available at: https://www.deeplearning.ai [Accessed 28 March 2025].
5. McKinsey & Company (2023) The state of AI in 2023: Generative AI's breakout year. Available at: https://www.mckinsey.com [Accessed 28 March 2025].
6. Schwab, K. (2016) The Fourth Industrial Revolution. Geneva: World Economic Forum.
7. Haenlein, M. And Kaplan, A. (2019) 'A brief history of artificial intelligence: On the past, present, and future of artificial intelligence', California Management Review, 61(4), pp. 5-14.
8. Gartner (2024) AI trends and predictions for 2025. Available at: https://www.gartner.com [Accessed 28 March 2025].
9. Bostrom, N. (2014) Superintelligence: Paths, dangers, strategies. Oxford: Oxford University Press.
10. Kaplan, J. (2016) Artificial intelligence: What everyone needs to know. Oxford: Oxford University Press.
11. Harvard Business Review (2022) How leaders can integrate AI into decision-making. Available at: https://hbr.org [Accessed 28 March 2025].
12. Microsoft (2023) Copilot and the future of AI-driven productivity. Available at: https://www.microsoft.com [Accessed 28 March 2025].
13. Huang, M.H. and Rust, R.T. (2021) 'Engaged or replaced? AI and the future of service', Journal of Service Research, 24(1), pp. 30-41.

14. Porter, M.E. and Heppelmann, J.E. (2014) 'How smart, connected products are transforming competition', Harvard Business Review, 92(11), pp. 64-88.

15. West, D.M. (2018) The future of work: Robots, AI, and automation. Washington, D.C.: Brookings Institution Press.

ABOUT THE AUTHOR

Silva Nash is a recognized thought leader in the field of artificial intelligence, leadership, and business strategy. With a background spanning 12 years in technology consulting, AI-driven business transformation, and executive leadership coaching, Silva Nash has worked with Fortune 500 companies, startups, and government organizations to integrate AI into strategic decision-making.

Beyond consulting, Silva Nash is a sought-after keynote speaker, sharing insights at global conferences and industry events on how leaders can harness AI to drive innovation and competitive advantage. Passionate about ethical AI, he advocates for responsible AI adoption that aligns with organizational goals while maintaining human oversight.

In this book, Silva Nashdi stills years of experience into a practical guide tailored for leaders who may not have a technical background but recognize the transformative power of AI. By breaking down complex concepts into actionable strategies, he aims to empower leaders to confidently navigate the AI revolution.